Silkie chickens or Silkies

Silkie Chickens as Pets

Silkie chickens book for care, behavior, diet, grooming, costs and health.

By

Martin Upton

Table of Contents

Introduction

Silkie chickens are great animals to have as pets. They are entertaining and useful. Raising them has become popular around the world. They are famous in poultry expos and contests and became the top show breed.

Are you thinking of taking the adventure of raising silkie chickens? Or maybe you have taken it already. You will discover that raising silkie chickens is both pleasant and entertaining.

Keeping silkie chickens takes a little time to satisfy their needs. You will have to ensure that they are happy, healthy and safe. If you provide them with good care, you will see how loving these beings are. You will admire their beauty and their cuteness.

If you are new to raising silkie chickens, you will enjoy the experience. Silkie chickens are inexpensive to raise and look after compared to most other pets. They will offer many years of companionship. It is a lovely surprise to the family.

This book will be your guide on how to raise silkies and care for them from the egg to the mature chickens. You will also find the answer to the frequently asked questions that a chicken owner can think of. So, get ready for the journey.

Chapter 1. Why keep silkie chickens?

The silkie chicken, or silkie in short, is a beautiful ornamental breed of chicken with a very special plumage. Their plumage looks fluffy and feels almost like silk, that's where the name silkie came from. The silkie chicken is one of the oldest chicken breeds that have been introduced to Europe from China in the 13th century. Soon after, this breed became popular and was introduced to the rest of the world and became the star of the chicken world.

In this chapter, we will explore the history of this breed, its varieties and what makes it popular among chicken lovers.

You may be wondering how many breeds there are. Well, there are so many of them. But first, what a breed is? A breed refers to an established group of animals that have the same morphological and genetic characteristics. These characteristics are identically transmitted to the consecutive progenies.

Domestic animals have far more breeds than their wild brothers' due to the human intervention and cross breeding that led to the creation of today's many breeds. Chickens also have so many breeds. There are several hundreds of chicken breeds across the world, but not all breeds are officially recognized. Chicken breeds differ in size, plumage color, skin color, comb type, egg laying potential and many other traits.

Chicken breeds

Chicken breeds can be divided into 5 categories based on their use. There are some chicken breeds that are raised for their meat, others for eggs, some others have a pet potential like silkie chickens.

The following list summarizes the most famous breeds of chickens and their uses. This is not an exhaustive list. There are way too many chicken breeds that can't be described in this book, but all of them fall in this classification.

- Egg-type breeds:

There are some chicken breeds that have high numbers of eggs produced per year. Those breeds are exploited in commercial laying farms to produce maximum egg numbers. The Rhode Island, the Leghorn and the Cornish are famous egg breeds.

Famous backyard egg breeds include the Ameraucana breed, Golden Comet, Hamburg, Lakenvelder and Sussex.

- Meat-type breeds:

Chicken meat breeds are also called broilers. They are famous for gaining a lot of weight in a short amount of time. This genetic trait is exploited in broiler farms to produce chicken meat on a large scale. There are many examples of broiler breeds like the Cobb, Ross, Arbor acres, Hubbard and Lohmann.

- Dual purpose breeds:

These are the breeds that are good layers. Examples include the Ancona, Catalana, Favaucana, Plymouth, Star, Light Brahma, Black Australorp, Barnevelder, Orphington, Java, Buckeye, Lamona, Legbar, Dorking and Langshan.

- Ornamental breeds:

Not all chickens are raised for their meat or eggs. Some chickens have a nice look with beautiful feathers. They are suitable for shows and beauty contests.

The silkie chicken breed is the most famous ornamental breed. Other examples include the Frizzled, Cochin, Japanese, Serama, Sebright, Antwerp, Mille fleur, Porcelain and Pyncheon. Google them to see photos!

- Game breeds:

These are the breeds that are used for competitions. Cock fighting is a famous chicken game. Game breeds are known for their pugnacity and their combative character. The Aseel breed is famous in this use.

Cockfighting is thought to be the first purpose for domesticating chickens and many people around the world still find it exciting.

Are silkie chickens right for you?

Silkie chickens have the same characters that an ideal pet would have. They are friendly, docile, and you can easily handle them and cuddle them.

Of course, they are not as smart as dogs are, but they have their own kind of intelligence, they are affectionate, entertaining and fun to handle and play with.

Silkie chickens are extremely safe and active. Overall, they are compact with short legs and roundish bodies, they are perfect to be raised in urban environments because they require less space and are easily adapted to live with humans and interact with them more than any other kind of chickens

Silkie chickens are very popular in pet shows, they have the best rankings over other breeds due to their amazing diversity of looks and colors. They are charming and spectacular. So, if you are fond of pet contests or willing to take part in poultry shows, then you must have your own silkie chickens!

Good show silkies must conform to the standards. The standards are created to encourage raising purebred silkies and protect them. The standard of perfection is explained later in this book.

Even if you do not want to show silkies, you can have your own pen of silkies that you will enjoy raising and looking after.

Silkie chickens have an unusual mother instinct that makes them perfect to raise chicks. You won't need to incubate eggs with a hatcher because the silkie hen will love to do the job naturally. You can raise silkie chickens with other breeds to incubate eggs for other hens and you will get new chicks more frequently.

Silkie chickens' history

Let's talk a little about history, which might not be your favorite subject in school, but even chickens have their own history!

Chickens are thought to originate from cold blooded reptiles around 50 million years ago. Believe it or not; chicken and reptiles are cousins! The common ancestor of all modern world chickens is the red junglefowl which is scientifically known as *Gallus gallus*. The junglefowl have a smaller size and run fast. They still have some of the primeval traits of chickens and fear humans. They still exist in southeast Asia in small number.

The modern chicken *Gallus gallus domesticus* is considered as a subspecies of the junglefowl. Recent studies proved that chickens were first domesticated in Asia around 8,000 years ago. They were first domesticated for entertainment purposes like cock fighting. Then they were raised as a source of meat and eggs.

It is believed that geographical isolation, as well as human intervention on chicken breeding, has led to the apparition of different breeds.

Silkie chickens are Chinese in origin. They were first introduced to Europe and the west countries with trade and were carried on the silk route. The first unambiguous record of the Silkie fowl was found in a Chinese book written in the 11th century.

In the 13th century, the famous traveler Marco Polo described silkie chickens with their fur-like feathers and black skin. He wrote in the book of the marvels of the world:

"I have been told, but did not myself see the animal, that there are found, at this place a species of domestic fowls which have no feathers, their skin being clothed with a black hair, resembling the fur of cats. Such a sight must be extraordinary. They lay eggs like other fowls, and are good to eat."

The silkie breed was later introduced to Europe and sold as the "Chicken Rabbit". In 1852, this breed was formally recognized in France. A few years later, it made its way to North America. In 1874, it was officially recognized as a breed.

Now, the silkie chicken breed ranks in the top 15 breeds in the United States. Many clubs and associations interested in the silkie breed were created as the number of silkie chicken keepers grew.

Myths around silkie chickens

Silkie chickens have been surrounded by myths for a long time in many parts of the world. In China, the silkie chicken has been thought to have medicinal values; Chinese women consume it after giving birth because she is believed to give energy and vivacity. It is thought also to have a curative effect on many diseases such as lung, stomach, and blood diseases. The silkie chicken meat is still consumed in China and some other countries.

Silkies bones were sold as powder. These powders were thought to have great medicinal powers. They were used in early medicine.

In ancient Europe, some breeders believed that this chicken was the result of a cross of a chicken with a rabbit! It was called the "chicken rabbit".

Silkie chicken varieties:

Silkie chickens come in many varieties. There are many plumage colors, slight variations in size as well as some distinctive marks on their bodies.

According to size, there are two types of silkie chickens: the standard silkies and the bantam silkies. Bantam means miniature chickens. Generally, bantam silkies are between 8-14 inches tall. They are commonly found in America. In other countries, their size is bigger. They are known as the standard silkies, which are 2 times bigger than bantam silkies.

Standard silkie hens weight around 2 pounds and cockerels can reach 3 pounds, while bantam silkie hens can be 1 pound and the male 1.2 pounds. Both varieties have a round body and they are feathered from the top of the face to the toes.

The most used classification is based on the appearance of the face feathers. There are bearded silkies and non-bearded silkies.

- Bearded silkies

As their names suggests, bearded silkies have head feathers that come all over their head and cover their wattles and earlobes. They have a full and fluffy beard of feathers around the bottom of their beak. The beard comes up under the beak and covers the crest and the face. The face is often invisible.

Chicks of the bearded variety hatch with no beard. They develop the beards when they grow older. If you don't know the chick's parents, it is hard to figure out if he will have its beard or not until he reaches several weeks old.

Most silkies in the United States are of the bearded variety. Most of the time, the feathers cover the silkies eyes making them unable to see well. So, face feathers must be trimmed or pinned.

- Non-bearded silkies:

Non-bearded or un-bearded silkies do not have dense feathers below their beak. Their eyes, wattles and earlobes are exposed. They tend to be more active because they don't have obstacle feathers on their face.

Non-bearded silkies have larger wattles than the bearded ones. The wattles are larger in cocks than in hens.

- Naked-neck silkies or showgirls

The naked-neck silkie is quite a new silkie variety. It has the feathers of a silkie chicken with a featherless neck. Naked neck silkies are not recognized as a breed because they are hybrid. It is the result of breeding silkies with the naked neck Turkey.

Facts about Silkie chickens

The silkie chicken is also called the Chinese silkie chicken or Bantam silkie. They are very hardy and have a good lifespan of about 9 years. It has some unique characteristics and a good personality that distinguish it from other chicken breeds. Below are the traits that make them distinct from the rest of their species.

Furry feathers

The most remarkable trait in silkie chickens is their distinctive fur-like feathers all over their body. Their feathers look so fluffy. They have been described as the "poodles" of the chicken world. Their feathers are as long as the feathers of any other chicken, but they are organized in a different manner.

If you look at a normal chicken feather of any other breed, typically you will find a series of hairs growing on both sides of the main shaft of the feather. These hairs are called barbs. The barbs are arranged and straight in a single feather. If you look closer, you can see that these barbs have tiny branches going from each barb. These are called barbules; these barbules are lined with tiny hooks called barbicels which keep the barbules attached to each other and that is what gives feathers their flat web.

Silkies lack the barbicels. Therefore, the barbules are not attached to each other. That's why every feather has a broken surface and looks like a duster. This is the secret behind their fluffy appearance and their softness.

Silkies also have additional feathers growing down their legs and over their toes. This feature is common in some other breeds like Brahma and Cochin.

The standard silkie feathers are all white. But today, there are many colors. This is the result of cross breeding with other chickens and mutations. The most common colors are white, brownish, blue, black, and golden, the standard acceptable colors in shows are the white, splash, black, blue, gray, buff and partridge.

There are many other color variations. Although these seem to be popular, they are not eligible to compete according to the standard of perfection in poultry shows. These colors are lavender, red, porcelain, and cuckoo.

Pentadactyl legs

Normal chickens' legs are composed of 4 toes and a spur; three toes that point forward and one toe that points backwards. Silkie chickens are famous for having 5 toes on each leg instead of four toes as in other breeds.

The additional toe grows above the back toe and just below the spur and it points upwards.

The 5 toe property is not specific to the silkie breed. Some other breeds also have five toes like Dorking, Faverolle, Houden, and Sultan.

This is a mutation and does not affect the silkie's walk. It is more of an adored characteristic that people love to see! But this number is not always the same in all silkies. In rare cases, there are some silkies that will have 4 toes or even 6.

Black skin and bones

Unlike most chickens, which have yellow or light pink skin, silkies have black skin. The black skin is common in all silkie chicken varieties, regardless of their plumage color.

The biological reason for this was not understood until recent studies that uncovered that this trait is the result of a genetic mutation.

Owing to this mutation, there is an increased synthesis of a pigmentary protein called melanin. Melanin is produced by many cell types in the body like the skin, the eyes, bones and heart. If produced in excessive amounts, melanin gives a black color to the organ. That's what gives the dark color of the skin, bones and internal organs in silkies. This condition is scientifically known as fibromelanosis.

She cannot fly

Silkie chicken can't fly that well. Well, you may be thinking that all chickens can't fly. But the silkie chicken is unable to fly even for a short distance, as other chickens do. In fact, normal breeds of chicken can fly for quite a long distance while running or when trying to reach high places to perch or to nest. Silkie chickens can't do any of that.

The fluffy plumage does not trap the air to lift the body. So even a short chicken wire can keep silkies in since they can't fly even for few feet. So, you won't have to worry about chickens patrolling your neighbors' yards.

On the other hand, Silkies cannot perch in high roosts where other chickens can reach. It is recommended to place perches low so they can get up and down effortlessly. If not, they will stick to each other in a pile and sleep on the ground.

The vaulted skulls

All silkie chickens have a hole in the top of the skull. The skull bone is not completely closed on the top. The vault sits right behind the comb and is believed to give a nicer elevation to the crest. There is some evidence among breeders that the vaulted skull in male silkies can improve the appearance of their crest.

The vaulted skull is a genetic trait that has been introduced via crosses with the crested Polish chickens to improve and create a larger crest. Breeding silkies with other breeds was very common in search of new colors, traits and types. This has been developed by the show poultry people who like a heavy crest.

Many breeders perform breeding to obtain a large crest, although it means to get a big vault in the skull. This is what gives them the domey head. Silkies with vaulted skulls are called round heads and others without are called flat heads.

This allows a part of the brain to protrude through it and this is what gives the visible knob above the head in chicks. This is known as the cerebral hernia, it is not only specific to silkie chickens and it is common in some other crested breeds. Not all vaulted skulls result in the hernia of the brain. In cases where breeding is selected to grow the size of the crest, a brain hernia is more likely to occur.

Cerebral hernia is not as bad as it sounds. Even if it is herniated, the brain remains covered with skin and feathers. However, in chicks, the knob is extremely sensitive. If he gets pecked on the head or gets smashes on its head, it becomes swollen and the brain gets compressed, this may result in neurological damage or can sometimes be fatal.

Sweet personality

Silkies have a quiet temperament. They are docile and love to interact with humans. Many people agree that silkies are the gentlest breed, although they are not considered the most intelligent.

Silkies get used to being handled and cuddled and become too attached to their caretaker.

Silkies make great pets for most people. They are quieter than other chickens. They love to spend their time looking for bugs and worms without messing up the garden.

Silkies interact well with other chickens and animals. Usually, silkies adjust to living with other pets like dogs or cats and build strong relationships.

Good mothers

Silkies brood remarkably well. It may be the top breed in the ranking of broodiness. Silkies often tend to go broody and they may sometimes be aggressive when protecting their offspring.

Although they are not good egg producers, Silkie hens can produce between 120-150 eggs per year. They love to sit on eggs and happily raise chicks. Many people use silkies to raise other chickens' breeds or even other fowl species. Silkie reproduction is extremely easy with natural incubation and has never been a problem for chicken keepers. Silkie hens can go broody several times per year. You will learn more about broodiness later in this book.

Chapter 2. Basics of chicken biology and behavior

In this chapter, you will find, in much greater detail, the basics of chicken biology; how chickens develop inside the egg, what chickens need to grow healthily, how they eat, drink and reproduce. Those details are necessary for any silkie chicken keeper. I know that biology is complex and boring, but it is necessary to understand the basic body phenomena.

You are probably going to find some competition from other silkie chicken keepers, so knowing a little more matters a lot! Let's first start by learning some terminology.

Some terminology

Chickens have many development stages; from hatching to the adult stage. There are many different terms that describe each age. A newly hatched bird is called a chick, that's too obvious eh? But for how long you will be calling it a chick? Not for too long. A chick is the young bird from the day he hatches until he loses his down feathers or the fluff.

The fluff is a very soft plumage that covers newly hatched birds and then it will be replaced by stronger feathers. This happens around six weeks of age, this may be more obvious in other breeds of chickens but in silkies, the transition may be unnoticed because of their soft plumage.

Young adult males are called cockerels or roosters. Many people call them cockerels until they reach one-year old. They are then called roosters.

The young immature female is called a pullet. The pullet begins laying eggs at the age of about 20 weeks in most of the breeds, but it takes more time for other breeds. Silkie hens usually start laying eggs between 6 and 8 months old. After her first egg, the pullet can be called a hen but many people continue to name it pullet until 1 year of age.

The capon is the castrated male of chickens, caponization is still in use in many areas around the world and its effects are related to fat deposition and muscle growth. Capons tend to have more muscles and their flesh has more fat. Capons are only an option for large meat chickens.

Chicken external parts

It may sound odd to focus on chicken parts in this chapter, but is useful to know the difference between males and females. Chicken's bodies are not too complex but have some differences from mammals. The chicken body is still primitive when compared to mammal's bodies, their organs are not so developed.

It is important to take a tour of the chicken body components and their functions to better understand how things happen in their bodies. We will start by learning a little about the chicken's anatomy. There are some anatomical differences between some breeds as well as between males and females.

The head sphere

The silkie head is small and is comprised of several parts: The beak, the comb, the wattles, the eyes and the earlobes.

- The beak

One of the most remarkable parts on the head is the beak. It is the equivalent of the mouth in humans. Chickens don't have teeth. The beak of silkies is often gray to dark blue in color. It has two nostrils in the upper half that are the chicken nose.

The beak's role is to pick up food and makes it ready to be swallowed. The beak has many other roles like preening and defense. Chickens use their beaks to groom themselves and distribute preen oil on their feathers. It is also used to scratch their skin trying to kill parasites.

Hatching chicks have a little sharp protuberance in the edge of the beak called the egg tooth. The egg tooth is used to peck at the egg shell to crack it. The egg tooth disappears when the chick gets older.

Normal chicken beaks should be smooth, sharp and slightly curved downwards.

- The comb

The comb is the upper part of a chicken head just above the beak. It is also called the crest. It is an enlarged skin tissue that has rich blood vessels. In silkies, the crest has a dark purple comb, unlike most chicken breeds where it is red in color.

Young silkie chickens have small pink combs. Combs become bigger in size as they grow up but they may become totally covered by head feathers.

The crest has an immense variety of shapes and colors in different breeds. Silkie roosters have walnut-shaped combs in mulberry color. Combs are usually larger on males than on females. It is a reliable sign of distinction between males and females and is also an excellent indicator of chicken health.

The comb's main role is to cool the chicken down in hot weather. Chickens don't sweat like many other animals do. Therefore, they use their comb and wattles to cool themselves down. As blood circulates through them, the heat is released and the body temperature cools down. This has little or nothing to do with silkie chickens because in silkies, the comb is very small. Does this mean that silkies do not fell comfortable in the heat? Well, yes, silkies have hard time staying cool in hot weather.

In breeds with large size combs, the comb has an attracting effect between males and females. Mature pullet combs are red and this attracts males who like red colors.

- The wattles

The wattles are a pair of skin lobes at the bottom of the beak. The wattles are small and always smaller in hens than in males. In bearded silkies, the wattles are covered with beard feathers.

In chicks, wattles appear earlier in males than in females, you can use combs and wattles to figure out the gender of the grown-up chicks by comparison of their crests and wattles as early as 2 months old.

- Sense organs

Silkie chickens have dark eyes with black, gray or brown pupils. Contrary to what many people think, chickens can see all the colors as well as some extra ones. Your silkies do see more colours than you do. They can see ultraviolet light. They have special retinal cones that can perceive ultraviolet radiations.

UV vision in birds was first demonstrated in hummingbirds and in pigeons and its function was not fully understood. It may be no more useful than asking the question "why do silkies see yellow"? Genuinely, there are some confirmed hypothesis that ultraviolet vision helps achieve many behaviours like foraging, signalling and sexual selection. So, it is helpful in spotting bugs in the grass!

Chickens have three eyelids on each eye. They have an internal eyelid that comes below the normal eyelids and it can be easily spotted if you take a close look to your chicken eyes. This is thought to protect flying birds' eyes from wind when there are at flight. In chickens, it is more like an additional wiper that moistens the eyes and protects them from dust.

Silkie ears are small holes found in each side of the head with skin lobes. The ear lobes may be blue or black. Ears are naked in non-bearded silkies whereas in bearded silkies they are totally covered in feathers.

The saddle, wings and tail:

The saddle corresponds to the area between the neck and the tail. This area is covered with feathers having varied sizes called contour feathers. There are 4 types of feathers in mature chickens: down feathers, contour feathers, semiplumes and filoplumes. Semiplumes are small feathers that grow between contour feathers and act as insulation. Filoplumes grow at the base of each contour feather.

Young chicks hatch with down feathers or fluff covering their skin, then they molt to grow new strong feathers.

Wings have many sets of feathers or rows. The larger feathers are called remiges and have 2 subtypes: the primaries and the secondaries. The primary feathers are those that grow at the extreme end of the wings. They are strong and large. Secondaries grow just behind the primaries and cover the forearm. Coverts are the next row of feather just above the primaries.

The tail has special feathers that point upwards. They are larger in males than in females. Hackle feathers are fine contour feathers that cover the neck and saddle. Feathers play an important role in maintaining body temperature.

Like all other breeds, silkies go through a molting process where they gradually lose their old feathers and new feathers will grow in their place.

This process happens once every year in mature chickens. New feathers take 4 to 8 weeks to fully grow. The molting chickens may look scruffy but it is completely normal for them, they are just changing their clothes.

The legs

From top to bottom, legs are composed of thighs, shanks, toes and claws. Thighs are connected to the shank at the hock joint which is the equivalent of the human ankle. Silkie shanks are covered with feathers.

Silkies have 3 toes projecting forward and two toes projecting backwards. Each toe ends with a sharp claw.

The vent

The vent, or cloaca, is the common orifice by which feces, urine and eggs are eliminated. The vent of silkie chickens are all covered with feathers. When the hen lays an egg, the vent protrudes and then it retracts.

Chicken inner parts

Digestive system

It is good to know chicken internal parts to better understand their functions. We will consider the digestive tract of the chicken, which begins from its beak and ends in the vent.

The chicken pecks food particles with its beak. Pecked food will be moistened with saliva produced by the salivary glands. After being swallowed, the food bowel travels inside the esophagus to reach the crop which is a temporary stomach that stores food and adds some chemicals to begin the digestion process.

You can feel the crop of a chicken by a gentle palpation in the base of her neck. If the chicken has just eaten the food, you can feel food particles through the skin. This procedure is often used to check if a chicken has eaten her food or not.

After a short stay in the crop, food is then passed into the lower esophagus to reach the proventriculus, which is the real stomach. The proventriculus has many glands that secrete digestive juices. The juices contains hydrochloric acid and enzymes.

Inside the proventriculus, the food bowl is mixed with hydrochloric acid. This starts the digestion of proteins. The acid content of the proventriculus serves to dissolve food minerals such as calcium salts and plays a role in killing pathogenic bacteria present in the feed. The proventriculus secretes mucus to protect its inner wall from the acid damage.

The food is then passed to the gizzard where it will be ground up. This is eased by the grit ingested. Mechanical digestion occurs in the gizzard. Then, the partially digested feed, known as chyme, moves from the gizzard to the gut.

The real digestion takes place in the intestines. The chyme is added with enzymes to obtain absorbable nutrients. The intestines can be divided into small intestines and large intestines. The small intestine connects the gizzard to the large intestine. This is where digestion is completed and nutrients are absorbed.

The small intestine is composed of 3 compartments: the duodenum, the jejunum and the ileum. The duodenum has glands that produce an alkaline secretion to protect the duodenal wall from the acidic content that comes from the gizzard.

The pancreas connects to the duodenum via the pancreatic canal. The pancreas secretes several enzymes that help the digestion like trypsin, lipase, and amylase. These enzymes break down carbohydrates, proteins and fats to smaller chemical structures ready to be absorbed.

The liver also helps digestion by secreting bile. The bile helps digest fats. It is diverted in the duodenal lumen via the bile duct.

The result of digestion are small chemical compounds that can be absorbed via the gut wall. These nutrients are monosaccharides, amino acids, and monoglycerides. The absorption of minerals and vitamins also takes place in the intestine. Nutrient absorption consists of the passage of digested elements to membranes of the intestine and then to the bloodstream.

The internal gut wall has a large area that ensures the absorption of nutrients with a tiny muscle layer that repeatedly contracts and relaxes, mixing the chyme and moving it towards the large intestine.

The chyme then passes to the large intestine, which consists of a colon, a pair of caeca, and the cloaca known as the vent. In the large intestine, microbial digestion of fibers and water absorption takes place. Some remaining nutrients are absorbed with water in the colon.

The ceca are a pair of blind-ended tubes that characterize birds and some other species. The single one of them is called caecum. The equivalent of the ceca in humans is the appendix whose inflammation needs surgery. Caeca in chickens plays a role in water absorption and it hosts a bacterial fermentation that leads to vitamin synthesis.

Finally, the indigested chyme is passed to the cloaca to be ejected as feces. Overall, it takes about 6 to 10 hours for food to pass completely through a chicken's digestive system.

Absorption is crucial to supply the body with nutrients and water. Once the nutrients arrive in the blood, they are carried to other parts of body to exert their functions. Nutrients serve to produce energy and support essential body functions like breathing, digestion, blood circulation and muscle movement, replacement of old cells, growth, reproduction and egg production.

Unlike many other farm animals, chickens lack an enzyme called lactase which helps the digestion of milk sugar. Therefore, most milk products are not suited for use in chickens' diets. A small amount of cheese or yoghurt cannot perturb their gut. If given in high amounts, they may cause diarrhea and make a perturbation to the caecum flora.

Respiratory system

The respiratory system of chickens plays a vital role in the body. It absorbs oxygen and expels the carbon dioxide. All body cells need oxygen to be active and they release carbon dioxide. Respiration plays other roles like decreasing the body temperature in hot weather.

The respiratory system of chickens is composed of nares or nostrils, sinuses, windpipe, two lungs, and air sacs. Air sacs are additional air containers that help achieve respiration. Chickens have 4 pairs of air sacs and one impair sac, these are found inside the chicken thorax and abdomen.

Unlike humans, chickens lack a diaphragm to inflate and deflate the lungs. Instead, the lungs are inflated and deflated with the air sacs.

Reproductive system

The reproductive tract involves the organs responsible for making eggs in hens and making sperm in cocks.

A rooster becomes sexually mature at 5 months. Males have 2 testes found in their belly and they produce sperm to fertilize eggs. Sperm takes 14 days to form. The cockerel's semen has around 5 billion sperm per ml. Once inside the hen's oviduct, several sperm typically enter the germinal disc. Only one fuses with the female ovum.

Some roosters are extremely fertile and create a maximum number of quality sperm; other roosters are less fertile and do not make enough good sperm. Many factors are involved in roosters' fertility like genetics, environment, and nutrition.

The hen's reproductive system can be divided into two components: an ovary and an oviduct. The ovary is the organ that holds all the future eggs that will be laid by the hen. It produces the egg yolk. Every hen is hatched with all the eggs she's ever going to have in her entire life stocked in the ovary as a bunch of grapes. The single one of them is called ovum. She'll lay those eggs for as long as she lives.

The egg yolk starts its journey from the ovary. It is detached and passes through the infundibulum. The egg yolk gets water and nutrients supplied from the hen's blood. The egg yolk is enclosed in the perivitelline membrane, on which is found the germinal disc. The egg white and membranes are then added in the magnum and the shell is formed in the uterus.

The number of eggs a hen lays over her lifetime is invariable. These eggs must be fertilized to produce baby chicks. Fertilization takes place in the infundibulum if there are spermatozoids. Next, the egg formation continues as for a non-fertilized egg.

The egg is finally transported to the cloaca where it is ready to be laid. The egg formation process lasts 25 hours. So even good layers can't make one egg every day. The number of eggs a hen lays is dependent on her breed, the lighting cycle, the season and her nutrition.

The pullet begins egg laying at around 20 weeks of age. In silkies, this may be a little delayed. Once she has laid her first eggs, she continues laying during many weeks of production and stops in molting periods. Some hens start laying before others and some lay more eggs than others.

Understanding chickens' behavior

The chicken behavior is the manifestation of internal processes that happen in the body or the result of external stimuli. In simpler words, it can be defined as the chicken response to internal and external signals. For example, if a chicken is thirsty, the drop of blood volume sends signals to the brain to push the chicken to seek water and drink. Similarly, if an animal is hungry, the decrease in the concentration of blood nutrients as well as the vacuity of the bowels make the brain signals hunger, thus the chicken expresses a food searching behavior.

The close observation of chickens is a key factor to understand their behavior. So, the more time you spend with your silkies, the more able you become to explain their behavior.

Communication and social behaviour

Chickens are precocial species. One-day old chicks can move, eat and drink on their own. Chicks can leave their nests within a day or two with their mums. Chicks hatch with their eyes open and covered with downy feathers.

The chick hatches with a well-developed brain and can make decisions like where to go and when to hide. He can form memories of his nest and his mother. The chicks can walk, find food and water and communicate to many other birds that hatch in the nest with their eyes closed and remain for a period in their nests, depending on their parents.

Soon after having hatched, chicks can rapidly learn about their environment such as which food is around and how to identify their mother.

Like all other chick breeds, silkies learn about their environment via imprinting. The young silky chicks learn to identify, approach and follow their mother to find food, shelter and warmth. Chicks show this type of learning within the first 48 hours in their life.

In brooding areas without parents, chicks learn to find food for themselves. This is thought to be an innate trait. So, they tend to imprint on one another. This may mean that they are not learning appropriately and is thought to have implications for their behavior later in life.

There is plenty of evidence that indicates that chickens are smart creatures. Scientists have discovered that birds are capable of processing thoughts more than any other mammal can. Further, chickens' brains can repair a significant amount of damage, unlike mammals.

Chickens understand the counting concept and can be trained to count items by giving them rewards. Sometimes chickens trick other birds, and even other animals. Chickens have a midrange on the intelligence scale of birds.

Chickens have good vision and the optic area that analyses vision is quite large. Vision is vital to chicken survival. Chickens can spot predators from a good distance away. They can learn to spot and avoid other predators quite quickly. There are chickens that can differentiate between different dogs and know whether they're friends or enemies.

Chicken eyes can spot tiny seeds or movement of bugs. Chickens interact with each other in many ways, such as through sounds. Chickens emit different sounds with different meanings.

- Chicken sounds

Chickens communicate with each other frequently using vocalization and gestures. Chickens vocalize quite often and make a wide range of voices. The major sounds are:

✓ Cackling:

Cackling or clucking is the sound that hens make after they lay an egg. This is a good indicator for new eggs in the coop. Sometimes, other hens can join the cackling. It lasts few minutes.

✓ Crowing:

It is the loud sound that roosters make. Roosters crow all day long and more often in the morning. This vocalization begins in roosters when they become mature. The crow is thought to be a rooster territorial message that he is the ruler of the brood.

✓ Chucking:

This is the quiet noise hens and roosters make to communicate with each other. It is thought to be a conversational vocalization and occurs all day long and is often perceived when chickens are digging.

- ✓ Calling sound

To indicate a good supply of food. When a hen is roaming and she finds feed parts, she makes a calling sound to her chicks to eat. Roosters also make a calling sound to hens. They will make a call and pick up a piece of food, drop it, pick it up again and so on. This is intended to get the girls paying attention and come over and eat that piece of food.

- ✓ Growling:

Growling is an alarming sound that nesting and broody hens make to warn who comes near them and they usually peck to defend their eggs.

- ✓ Squawking:

Chickens emit this sound when they feel frightened. Some chickens make this sound when they are held and this is an alarming sound for other chickens to run away.

- • Dominance

Chickens like living together. They love companionship and they entertain special relationships with each other in the same flock.

Wild chicken form small flocks with 10 to 15 birds. In each wild flock, there is a rooster. Young male roosters are generally discarded by the dominant rooster. There is a sort of social ranking between hens. This ranking is determined by squabbling and fighting. The dominant hen has some privileges in food and nests. They eat first and lay in the best nests.

In managed flocks with enough space like backyard chickens, the hens are generally calm and fight rarely. Normally, the lowest on your pecking order will be bullied by other chickens, besides the rooster.

Roosters within the same flock have their ranking too. If there are many roosters, young roosters without hens will fight to get their ranking. The presence of hens makes them fight more often and the fight may end in a lot of injuries to roosters. Losers stay at the edge of the flock and keep a low profile. That's why it is necessary to keep good roosters and discard extra males from the flock. Silkie roosters do not support fighting and they may die of head injuries if they get hit hard on the top of their head.

A rooster always has the hens in his realm. He doesn't like hens squabbling among the flock. If squabbling among hens occurs, he may break up fights. The rooster protects his flock. Roosters tend to have a favorite hen, usually the dominant hen in the flock but they treat all hens well. And tend to mate with her more frequently.

- Interaction with other animals

Due to the fluffiness, silkies can seem strange to other domestic animals. Silkies don't often mix well with other pets like dogs, cats and ferrets.

✓ Interaction with dogs and cats

Dogs usually ignore chickens. But for some playful dogs, chickens are just fun. If the dog feels bored and wants to play with silkie chickens, he gets excited to chase them. Even if he doesn't hurt them, dogs are very stressful to chickens and sometimes injuries occur. Some dogs can be a deadly enemy for chickens but others cope well with chickens. Dogs' temperaments vary and can be unpredictable. That's why some precautions must be taken if chickens are kept with dogs. Be very careful when letting dogs and chickens together in the yard. Any dog breed is capable of doing harm to chickens. It is essential to watch the dog interacting with the chickens.

If chickens get stressed they may not lay eggs well and become more prone to getting sick. So, if your dog is causing problems, you must train him not to approach them, or simply manage an area for him where he can't reach the chickens. Always be cautious when your silkies are left along with dogs. If the dog hurts one of your chickens, don't get angry at him, he was just playing and didn't mean to cause harm. Take your silkie to the vet and think how to prevent this next time.

Cats don't pose a risk to adult chickens as they can defend themselves. Some cats are reported to kill chicks or eat them. So, you must ensure that no cat is allowed near the chicks. Silkies are most at risk because of their size and their inability to fly.

With the increasing habit of indoor silkies, cats have learned to live with silkies and sometimes they try to play with them. But this often is a love from one side and silkies often peck cats. With time, they can get more open to cats and they may interact with them a little.

    ✓   Silkies and Other Fowl species

Silkies do get along well with other chicken breeds, ducks and geese. They get used to other chicken breeds and make friends very quickly. But sometimes, silkies are bullied by other chickens. However, despite their small size, silkie chickens tend to dominate other chickens' breeds.

The dominance in mixed breed flocks depends on a lot of variables. Keep in mind that even if you want to mix silkies with other chickens, always ensure that silkie number is higher than other chickens and discard aggressive chickens. To minimize dominance, provide a lot of space and roosts to help reduce the crowd. Providing enough food for everyone is also necessary.

The best way to mix silkies with other chickens is to raise other breeds with silkies since a young age. Since they have grown up together, they will get along well with each other.

For other backyard birds like ducks and geese, ducks and geese don't get along well with silkie chickens. Competition about food may be a big problem, so ensure silkies are fed alone to avoid dominance. Moreover, male ducks can aggressively mate with silkie hens if they're deprived of their own females. For chicks, it is recommended not to mix silkie chicks with other birds' chicks because this may lead to more disease problems.

Feeding behavior

Silkie chickens are omnivorous. They explore their environment and eat vegetation, bugs, worms, seeds, fruit, meat and waste from human food. They will pick through the feces of other domestic animals for undigested grains and scratch up compost piles looking for nuggets.

Chickens are diurnal; they are active in the day and sleep in the night. Chickens exhibit specific behaviors in response to their real-time needs and their environment. So, if a chicken is hungry, she seeks food. And if she feels she will be laying an egg, she nests and so on. If chickens are given free access to the backyard, they spend nearly the third of the day pasturing and foraging. They look for edible items.

Chickens often pick up small rocks or pieces of gravel, which help them break down food in the gizzard. When they roam freely in the yard, they get plenty of grit. If they are confined, you may need to provide it. There is chicken grit available in pet stores.

Chickens have a weak sense of taste because they have few taste receptors. Sometimes chickens don't know what is OK for them to eat and what isn't. They like to eat shiny things because they think they are sand particles. Many chickens can eat bizarre things like metal objects or plastic things. So be careful if your yard contains any harmful objects, they may and up in your chicken crop and can be lethal for them.

Chickens also have a particular drinking mechanism; they open their beaks, grab some water and lift their beaks to let the water pass to the crop. This process is eased by gravity.

If food is abundant, chickens may have periods of rest in the hot weather. Chickens don't eat while they're in the dark and turn to sleep.

Preening and dustbathing

Preening and dustbathing are grooming behaviors in chickens that help to keep the skin and feathers in good condition. Silkies spend a lot of time looking after their feathers. There are 2 main interesting behaviors to keep feathers in good shape: preening and dustbathing.

Preening is the distribution of preen oil over the feathers; preen oil is a substance secreted from glands in the skin located in the base of the tail. The chicken uses her beak to pick up oil from the preen gland and then she distributes it over her plumage. She repeats these steps to distribute the preen oil across the plumage. This helps to make the plumage waterproof.

Silkies exceptionally hate getting wet and love to do a dust bath. If you provide a dusty area, chickens will bath frequently. Chickens prefer dry soil, sand or wood shavings to dust bathe. They scratch out a hole in the sand the size of their bodies and lay in it. They throw the sand from the hole into their feathers and then they shake to remove it.

Chickens dust bathe daily for about 10 minutes and this happens usually in the afternoon. This habit helps to control parasites. Silkies will really appreciate a box of sand to bathe in. They perform dust bathing to remove old preen oil from the plumage to keep feathers fluffy and improve the insulation of feathers.

Sleeping

Total darkness makes chickens go to sleep. They're most vulnerable to predators when they are asleep; most losses of chickens occur at night because most predators prowl these areas at that time and hunt chickens.

Because of the darkness, chickens don't defend themselves or try to escape. Before getting to sleep, they roost as high as they can to avoid predators. Silkies perch in low roosts since they can't fly to reach high sites.

Chickens get the habit of perching in the same place every night. The sleeping area should be calm and secure for silkies, otherwise they will try to choose their own perches. It is recommended to manage a sufficient perch for all chickens to sleep and ensure the coop is well protected against predators.

Chickens don't seem to sleep when the light is on, but in fact they make episodes of hemispheric sleep or one eye sleep as well as two eyes sleep. There are even birds than can sleep while flying. Sleep is not necessarily accompanied by eye closure.

Sleep may occur with the eyes wide open. This is thought to help them escape predators, since chickens are most vulnerable to predators at night..

Molting

You probably know a little about molting in chickens or maybe not. Many people don't know about molting until the time they see their chickens lose feathers. The first time they see it, they think it is a skin disease or a parasitic infection but it is not. This is a natural phenomenon of feather replacement that happens every year.

Chicken molting occurs gradually from the head feathers to the rest of the feathers. Chicks molt twice before maturity. The first molt begins at 6-8 days and lasts until 4 weeks. The down feathers are replaced by the first feathers. The second juvenile molt occurs at 7-12 weeks that's when second feathers replace the first ones. At that time, the difference between males and females can be observed. After that, molting occurs normally every fall for mature chickens

Old chickens begin annual molts after they reach 16-18 months. Throughout molting, old feathers are lost and new ones grow. This process requires a lot of protein to make feathers, that's why egg production drops because diet proteins are prioritized in growing new feathers. This takes about 8 weeks to finish.

Molting can happen unusually as a response to stressful conditions for chickens like an interruption of water supply or food shortage or a sudden change in lighting condition.

Like all chickens, silkies produce small debris and dust when their feathers are still growing. Dust is the result of feather debris that comes off when the shafts flake off as they grow out. The coop bedding will be messy with feathers but this will not last too long.

It is important to distinguish molting from feather plucking; in broody hens, or in hens that are bullied by roosters. There may be a focal loss of feathers. This is not a molt.

Courtship and mating

Many silkie chicken behaviors are controlled by hormones. So adult cockerels behave differently to immature male ones. This is due to testosterone which contributes to male behaviors like tenacity, aggression, vocalizations, mating behavior, and territoriality. Female chickens' behaviors are affected by estrogen. Therefore, they show more activity, feather-pecking and broodiness.

Chickens have a rapid courtship ritual. When a rooster wants to mate with a hen, he usually approaches her and may do a mating dance, he drops his wing and turns around her a few times until she submits or runs away. If the hen is ready to mate, she crouches down and moves her tail to one side as a sign of acceptance.

During mating, the rooster jumps on the hen's back, holds few feathers from the back of her neck with his beak and rapidly pushes his cloaca against her a few times. After that, he fluffs his feathers and walks away. The hen then stands up, fluffs her feathers and walks away. She may preen her feathers after mating. Note that a rooster may mate a hen even if he is infertile, so exhibiting the mating behavior is not a sign of male fertility.

Mating behaviour in roosters starts at 4 or 5 months old. But if there are dominant roosters around, this behaviour may start later. Mating can be done at any time during the day. Like all other breeds of hens, silkie hens don't need a rooster to lay eggs. Fertility is known to drop with the rooster's age and when the weather gets cold.

If the number of hens is low per rooster, the male will over-breed the hens, causing stress on them and sometimes pluck off their saddle feathers. It is important to increase the sex ratio to reduce this problem or change the male.

Nesting and brooding behaviours

Silkie hens are famous for their frequent broodiness. They have a good instinct to incubate eggs and hatch them. A broody hen ceases laying and remains sitting on eggs to incubate them. The instinct is too strong that the hen remains sitting even if there aren't any eggs.

The behavior of making the nest is induced by hormones. Usually a broody hen will start by making a nest in a quiet, dark spot. The hen looks for nest material and sets up a nest with her beak in the coop or in the garden, if chickens are kept free range, for a short time each day. She will start carrying bits of straw and feathers to line the nest and she will even pluck her own feathers from her breast to keep her eggs warm.

The hen will spend all her time there. She fluffs up her feathers to make herself bigger to cover the eggs. She often becomes aggressive defending her nest. She growls and grumbles at anyone who comes near her. She may even give pecks if you try to grab the eggs.

Hens can go broody even without a rooster in the pen. She remains incubating them unknowing that they will never become chicks. The hen then becomes less active and only leaves her nest to eat or drink. She may take quite a long time setting and thinking that the eggs are still to hatch. The hen becomes too weak and may lose feathers. This may seem sad, especially when the eggs are not fertile.

Chapter 3. What are the costs

Chickens are inexpensive to maintain. This does not mean to neglect the costs. A small flock may be cheap to maintain but when the number of chickens gets bigger, the cost will certainly increase. To be labelled as pets, your flock shouldn't exceed 10 chickens in your household.

Keeping silkies as pets implies providing a good, happy life for every single individual. A good estimation of the cost consists of making a full list of the equipment and tools needed to set up the housing and maintain the flock. The list should include the equipment, tables of food, electricity and litter and even estimates of the insurance and trucking costs.

The cost is flexible and depends on how you intend to raise your chicks as well as how sophisticated the housing and the equipment will be. There will be some one-time costs for keeping silkie chickens and some ongoing costs. One-time costs include housing and equipment. Ongoing costs include food, bedding, water and electricity if you want.

Chicken purchase

Silkie chickens are in high demand but the cost of buying silkies won't break your budget. An adult silkie hen price can range from $10 to $30 / £5 to £30. The price for hens that match show standards may be higher and it may reach $200 / £150.

Silkie chicks cost between $5 to $15 / £3 to £10 each. But sometimes you can even get free silkies from friends or neighbours. It is important that you keep a small pen of chickens that you can afford to feed and devote the right amount of time to clean their coop. Before you intend to buy some silkie chickens, you must provide good housing.

Housing and fencing costs

Housing costs may be variable. If you intend to raise chickens in the yard with free range most of the time, then your costs will be very low. If you want to build a fancy coop with a large outside run, your cost may rise to several hundreds of dollars.

A beautiful coop for chickens is affordable and lasts for years. A simple prebuilt coop for a few chickens ranges between $200 and $1000 / £150 to

£800. This price may be higher if you look for a better-quality coop. There are plenty of models of chicken coops that you can find online. You should keep in mind that the coop has a maximum capacity of chickens.

Building a chickens' coop from scratch is not an arduous task. All you need are some wood plates, bars, chicken wire, and some creativity. Keep in mind that there are some rules to apply when designing the coop like the minimal square feet per chicken as well as the number of nests and roosts.

Housing also requires some furnishings like feeders, waterers, roosts and nest boxes. For 5 chickens, these items will cost less than $50 / £40. There are some other items that you can optionally provide inside the coop like lighting.

The bedding cost should also be calculated; wood shavings will cost no more than $10 monthly. So, costs are extremely variable and range from $200 / £150 to even more than $400 / £300. This depends on how decorative the coop will be. I recommend that you make your own list of equipment and inquire about the costs from sellers and online stores and make your estimation of the costs.

You may need to set up an outside run for your silkies. This can be done with chicken wire on an area of the garden. The chicken netting is not too expensive. A galvanized chicken wire netting of 50 feet will cost less than $30/£25.

Feed costs

You can choose to feed your chickens commercial feeds or feed them seeds, grains and home-made diets. Commercial chicken feeds are recommended and are not expensive compared to dog and cat food.

It is estimated that the cost of feed for five silkie hens is less than $20 / £15 per month.

There are many categories of chicken feeds that are designed for every life stage of backyard chickens. Chicks should be fed the starter chicken feed until 6 weeks old. Then they should be fed the grower chicken feed until 20 weeks old and finally the layer chicken feed. Their prices may vary.

To estimate the costs, an adult silkie chicken eats around 1.2 to 1.5 lbs. of feed per week. So, if you have 10 adult chickens, then a 25 kg / 50 lbs. Bag of food will be enough for them for one month. For chicks, the average food consumption is about 7-9 lbs. Per bird in the first 10 weeks. A 50 lbs. A bag of chick starter crumbles will cost you around $15 / £10.

Feed costs are variable. A chick starter feed cost varies from $1 to $3 / £1 to £2 for the single pound of food and depends on the composition and the manufacturer. One pound of the laying hen feed costs the same as well as the grit. So, as a rule of thumb, a single chicken will cost around $10 / £8 in her first year and $20 to $40 (£15 to £30) per year in the other years.

Don't be scared by these calculations! They are calculated on a yearly basis. Moreover, feeding chickens has the reward of getting free eggs! So, the cost may be null since a silkie may produce 100 eggs within a year! That's around $40 / £30! And voilà, silkies are spending their own money! The diet should also contain free grass, bugs, and veggie scraps. These will help reduce the costs.

Insurance

Insurance for backyard chickens is not as common as conventional pet insurance. It is rare that people ever think of enrolling their chickens in pet insurance plans. Few insurance companies offer chicken insurance. The question is: is there a real need for chicken insurance?

Insurances main advantage is to get a great discount in veterinary bills. In chickens, veterinary costs are almost the same as cats or ferrets in emergencies. The price is not expensive and doesn't exceed several dollars per month. However, chickens don't get sick that often. Many people see that enrolling chickens in insurance programs is non-sense since they can afford to treat them. Besides, chickens don't require expensive care like dogs or cats.

On the other hand, owning chickens in the backyard may mean paying an extra amount of money in your homeowners insurance. This is meant to cover any accidental damage that may be caused by the pets. This may seem odd, because chickens can't do any harm to your home furniture nor pose a threat to people in the house. Many people don't declare owning chickens in the backyard.

Veterinary costs

Veterinary costs are unexpected costs and can't be calculated in advance. Most of the costs will be covered by the insurance, if you enroll in one. But even without insurance, chicken vet bills are often cheaper than dogs and cats.

Chickens don't get sick that often. But, injuries and diseases can occur even if your silkie chickens are kept in the safest environment. An ordinary vet visit for a sick chicken is around $25 / £20 but this is a minimal fee. Diagnostic tests may be needed like an x-ray or ultrasound. This will increase the bill. Drug costs may reach to $30 / £22 or more.

Chapter 4. Preparing for a flock

After successfully working out the costs, you can now move to bringing your new silkies to the yard. Before you get your new family members, you must consider all the things your silkie chickens will require of you: nutrition, money, safety and so on. All these tasks will be covered in this chapter.

Dealing with laws and regulations

It is a good habit to make plans for any project in life. Raising chickens is also a small project that needs good planning even if you intend to raise a small flock. The proverb says: "A goal without a plan is just a wish". So, a successful silkie keeper is a successful planner.

The very first step before raising chickens is to check regulations. As you may know, legal and regulatory requirements may apply in some cities and suburbs. But if you live in the countryside, then regulations may not pose any obstacle to your goal.

Many countries have put a set of rules to organize chicken keeping in urban areas to avoid problems associated with chicken keeping in backyards. In the past, chicken keeping was popular and there have been many problems associated with it like cockerel crowing and bad odors.

The regulations differ from one country to another and there may be some restrictions on the maximum number of chickens allowed per household. Generally, no more than 10 chickens are allowed in residential areas. You can find out the exact backyard animal housing restrictions in your area by contacting your city or state government office.

Many cities across the world require a permit or license to keep chickens in the backyard. These licenses can be taken from a permitting authority which may be the city animal control office or the public health department.

There may be regulations on how a coop should be built, dimensions and the maximum height for the structure. Some cities require a certain distance for a coop to be built away from other residences. This distance may range from several feet to several hundred feet. Cleaning and maintenance schedules may also be specified. There may be also requirements about managing windows if possible and prohibiting keeping chickens in cellars.

In the US, every city and local region has its unique set of laws and ordinances regarding pets keeping. Major cities allow raising chickens in backyards like New York, Los Angeles, Chicago and Houston. There are rules that limit the number of chickens. So, to avoid getting in trouble, you must not exceed the allowed number of chickens.

In the UK, there are regulations that prohibit chicken keeping. You should first check with your local council to see if there are any local by-laws that prevent chicken keeping in the backyard. If your property is rented, you must check the deeds or directly ask the landlord whether it is ok to raise chickens.

You should be careful not to disturb your neighbours and keep the area where chickens live clean to avoid any attention. If you don't know what your neighbours attitude is towards chickens, it is recommended to inform them before you start the pastime. Most of the concerns are about noise, vermin and odors. You should think how to deal with these issues from the beginning and this book is all about that!

A good check of regulations is extremely helpful in choosing the coop location and for setting things once for all. Once this step is done and you've got the green light, it is good to discuss the project with your family members, as they will be your partners in this project.

Starting with chicks or chickens?

Many new chicken keepers ask this question. If it is your first experience with raising chickens, it is advisable to start with adult chickens because they require less care and resist well to diseases. Plus, adult chickens produce eggs and you can expand your flock in no time. Just incubate some eggs and you will get chicks some weeks later.

Starting with chicks may be a tough task. Extra care must be taken. Chicks are sensitive and require more attention. They are very sensitive to the environment temperature. If chicks are too young, you must provide a warm environment for them and feed them appropriate food.

Anticipating silkie chicken needs

Before starting to raise silkie chickens, it is important to keep in mind that chicken keeping requires responsibility and commitment. To raise chickens appropriately, you must understand the basic needs of chickens.

Chickens need a good shelter with the appropriate equipment, a balanced diet, fresh water, and proper environment conditions including temperature, humidity and lighting. These will be fully explained further in this chapter.

Chicken nutrition is a key factor that conditions their growth and health. The silkie diet is not the same for every stage of life. There are some variations that should be taken in food composition and will be explained in the chapter about nutrition.

Silkie chickens are extremely sensitive to their external environment. So, make sure they don't get stressed. Silkie chickens are affectionate creatures and love cuddling and care. Beside basic care, chickens also need to be monitored to prevent diseases and perform deworming.

Living area requirements

You should decide where to place the coop in the yard if there is enough space. The coop should be protected and placed in a shady area if possible to avoid hot sun.

If you don't want problems with neighbors, simply don't place it too close to the fence. Chickens crowing can make neighbors annoyed and they can even make complaints to the police. This may ultimately cause eviction of the pen.

Having a coop alongside a fence has its advantages as long as it does not cause any conflicts with your neighbors. Many people make the fence a part of the chicken coop itself. This can act as a wind break and at certain times of the day the fence will provide shade.

Coops under trees, are also a good choice. The trees can protect from the sun and minimize winds. Some people use the garden shed for chickens. With a few adjustments, the garden shed can easily be changed into a chicken coop.

The chicken coop must be predator proof. This implies isolation from harsh weather conditions as well as rodents. It must be well designed and well decorated, the housing could be bought from pet supply stores or it may be as simple as a shelter made with treated lumber or a combination of pieces of metal, wood and wire.

You can design your own coop but you should keep in mind that it must be easy to clean and stands against the harsh weather. Common coops are made from wood bars and galvanized netting. Next are some important points to consider before starting the assembly:

✓ Adequate space:

The chicken coop area must be adapted to the number of chickens to be raised in it. The coop should have sufficient space for chickens to move, perch and dust. The area is a principal factor in chicken welfare. The area should ideally be 4 square feet of coop space per chicken.

The coop should also provide sufficient roosts and nests. The roosts should allow all chickens to perch. The number of nests should also permit all hens to lay; as a rule of thumb, the nest number should be no less than the third of the hens. So, for example, if you have six chickens, you can manage 2 or 3 nest boxes.

✓ Minimal height:

The chicken coop height does not really matter as much as the area. It is recommended that the roof should be tall enough so chickens can perch and reach their nests, the height should also allow you to get inside the coop to feed chickens and clean it.

✓ Water proof floor and roof:

Ideally a chicken coop should have a cement floor and washable walls. This would allow the coop to be well cleaned and disinfected when needed. The roof should not allow rain to get inside the coop.

✓ Renewable bedding:

The bedding should be easy to replace and clean. A clever idea consists of using large plastic trays on the floor as removable litter that can be filled with wood shavings. This is meant to make the bedding replacement easy.

If you can't provide trays, you can pour the wood shaving directly on the floor and replace it regularly. Keep in mind that the bedding should always be dry. The wet litter is very bad for chicken's legs.

✓ Dust boxes

Chickens love to take a dust bath. This helps them keep their feathers clean and smooth. If they don't have an outside run, a dusting box must be provided for chickens to do their favorite hobby. A dusting box must be far taller and wider than a chicken, it must be deep enough to permit a chicken to completely fit in. It must be filled with sand or fine wood particles.

✓ Outdoor run:

The chicken coop must have a small entrance that allows chickens to leave and come to the coop. This would make chickens more comfortable as they love moving about and digging in the garden.

The outdoor run should be well fixed in chicken wire or hardware cloth to prevent access of predators and wild birds as they may pose a threat in introducing and transmitting diseases to the pen.

To avoid the predator threat, you should allow chickens in and out yourself to keep the coop safe. There are some automatic door openers available on the market that allow chicken movements and prevent predators for about $150.

✓ Ventilation:

Ventilation is extremely important in renewing air and making the litter dry and minimize odors and dust. It plays also a role in cooling the coop. Ventilation's first purpose is not oxygenation since oxygen exchange can be made through tiny holes.

It is important to keep in mind that ventilation should be given in the right amount. The coop should resist to violent wind that can carry dust and bugs which may cause respiratory diseases. It is ideal to have your coop surrounded by trees or near fences. If not, a simple solution consists of fixing a tarp on the chicken coop when the wind is violent.

Ventilation plays a role in evacuating ammonia, which is a gas that comes with chicken droppings and is harmful to the chicken respiratory system in high levels.

Ventilation has a poor outcome in winter since the atmosphere is humid. Humidity in excess is detrimental for chickens as well, as it helps develop molds and fungi. If the weather is hot, a fan can be used to cool the coop. It can be purchased from pet supplies stores.

A common problem that silkie caretakers face is the tradeoff between ventilation and temperature in the cold weather; if you increase ventilation, the coop gets cold, and if you minimize it to keep the coop warm, then humidity increases.

✓ Equipment

Basic equipment of the coop are feed containers, water containers, roosts, and dust boxes.

There are many types of feed containers. The most commonly used ones are PVC tube feeders, hanging feed dispensers, galvanized tread-plate feeders, or simply feed pans can be used. The commercial feeders have the advantage of minimizing the waste of feed.

Drinkers are not the same for chicks and chickens. If chicks are kept with their mum, you must ensure that chicks have access to drinkers placed on the floor. Hanging drinkers or water containers with nipples are hard for chicks to reach. But chicks will learn quickly to pick the nipples to drink.

Commercial coops have their perches included. But if you are planning to build your own coop, perches can be made as a series of wooden bars fixed to the coop wall. Their number must permit all the chickens to roost.

You can provide a big plastic dish or a wooden box filled with dust as a dust box. If chickens are allowed outside the coop, they may also dust bathe in the garden.

The nests are totally made from wood because of its good at thermal insulation. This means that the temperature inside the nest remains warm and doesn't get affected by the outside temperature.

Temperature and lighting

Chicken's ancestors lived in tropical and subtropical areas. They are native to the hot climate of south Asia. They can very well adapt to cold climates and need protection from extreme weather conditions.

Adult chickens are warm blooded, they can keep their body temperatures within the range of 105-107°F. Chickens have a comfort zone for temperature in which the body thermoregulating mechanisms are at rest. Chicken thermal comfort zone in the coop is between 50-68°F and can adapt to temperatures up to 77°F. In cold weather, the chicken body continuously produces heat to keep the chicken alive.

When the weather is hot, the body tries to disperse heat through rapid respiration and using the comb and wattles as a cooling pads. The inability to sweat and the small size of their comb and wattles makes it difficult for chickens to adjust to extreme hot weather. Above 100°F, chickens suffer a heat stress; they drink a lot of water and pant to cool down.

Observing the chickens will determine how they feel in the heat. A fan or a cooling pad in the coop will be a good solution. A good keeping practice is the use of thermometers with minimum and maximum memory of both temperature and humidity inside the chicken coop.

The coop should protect chickens from the extreme cold weather. Cold weather is detrimental for chickens and especially chicks. Heil and ice pellets can cause frostbites in the comb and toes. These lesions are incurable and the tissue is permanently damaged. So, if the weather is too cold, the chicken coop should be covered with a tarp or move the chickens to a safer place.

Beside temperature, Chickens are dependent on daylight. Chickens love to move about in the sun, so manage a sunny corner in their coop. Daylight periods influence most of the chicken's behavior as well as egg production. Avoid placing your chicken coop in dim light or completely closed areas. The coop walls should also permit a good amount of light to enter the coop.

Chickens reared in yards tend to lay fewer eggs in short day seasons. This is due to the decrease in daytime length. Chickens do not prefer to incubate eggs in the winter since there will be hard times for chicks to survive.

Hens can get back to their normal laying using artificial light. If you apply 16 hours of light for hens, they will continue to lay, thinking that this is the long days season. In layer hen farms, artificial lighting with special intensity and spectrum is used. Timed power dimmers are used to control lighting.

Artificial lighting is not necessary in silkie chickens. Silkie chickens are not good layers. If you want to get more eggs, simply add more hens rather than expanding the duration of light exposure.

Setting up housing for chickens

To set up housing for your chickens, you need to examine all the possibilities that you can create in your yard and how to provide a sufficient space for them. You may be limited by the space in your backyard. But the chicken coop needs a minimal space per chicken, proper ventilation and lighting, as discussed before. These conditions are set to guarantee welfare for chickens as well as to minimize diseases that result from overcrowding.

The minimal area of the coop is dependent on the maximum number of chickens you want to keep. We advise not to raise so many chickens; no more than one male and several females. Whether you intend to build or buy a chicken coop, the coop should have a minimal square footage that allows no less than 2 square feet per bird with free access to the garden. Silkies need space to stand, turn around, lie down and move freely.

The square footage can be as wide as 15 square feet per bird. The more space provided the better the chickens will behave. If there is not enough space, chickens get overcrowded and they may fight more and get their feathers damaged and this is unacceptable for show silkies.

It is obvious that a chicken coop will need a door with lock, windows to let the air in and out, and if it is possible, a small door for the chickens to let them come and go freely to the yard, unless there is a threat from predators. Inside the coop, place feeders and drinkers and a mini dirt puddle filled with sand or wood shavings.

Chicken coops are available for sale online. The price of a simple wooden chicken coop ranges from $100 to $300. It suitable for a small number of chickens of less than 10.

If you are willing to build your coop, all you need is a bit of imagination and handcrafting. The coop should be robust and resist wind and rain. You will need some metal bars, chicken netting, wooden plates, and some tools to do the assembly.

Many silkie owners prefer to keep the silkies as house pets. This may not be safe for humans, unless you keep high biosecurity for you and your family. The CDC biosecurity recommendations state not to eat or drink where the chickens live or roam and not to wash their bowls in the kitchen sink. It prohibits housing poultry in bathrooms or keeping them where food is prepared, served or stored.

Buying silkie chickens

Before buying a couple of silkie chickens, you must know few things before buying. If you planning to participate in poultry shows, then not all types of silkies are accepted in shows. In shows, ranking is based on some criteria that the chickens must have, referred to as the standard of perfection.

To purchase a model silkie you must check the parents' traits to increase your chances of winning. There are some silkie keepers that devote their spare time to breeding silkies that have highly selected traits that meet the standards.

The price of these chickens may be higher but if you own purebred silkies, you will obtain brilliant competitive chicks. Pet quality silkies can be purchased from breeders that participate in shows and select silkies for that purpose. Most of these owners are member of associations of silkie chickens' breeders.

If you plan to raise silkies for your own pleasure, you can find some chickens from another silkie keeper. There are many ways someone can get some silkie chickens; someone who keeps silkies in his backyard, a neighbor, feed stores, farmer's market, or you can make an order from online stores. But regardless of the type of silkie or the variety you are looking for, you must ensure that the silkies are in good health. Here are some tips:

- The silkie should be active and walks properly with no leg injuries. Inspect the legs for the number of toes as this is hereditary.
- The feathers should be fluffy and in good shape. Inspect the skin under the feathers for external parasites or sores.

- The eyes should be clear with no discharge or swelling.
- The nostrils should be clear with no scabs or crusts or discharge. The chicken should breath through her nostrils.
- The legs should be clear and the leg skin should be clear with no scales or thickening.
- The feet should be clear and not covered in droppings and without any wounds.

When buying your first chickens or when you intend to add one chicken or expand the flock size, it is highly recommended that you keep the newly bought chicken in a separate area. Give him water and food for at least one week. This step is called quarantine and is meant to check for diseases and protect your flock from getting contaminated by diseases.

Once the chicken is good enough in eating and behaving normally, then you can transfer her to the rest of the flock. This procedure is so often neglected and unfortunately, it is a common disaster for chicken owners that led them to lose some of their chickens after adding a new member to the flock without quarantine.

When you are buying your first flock, remember to respect the number of roosters per hen. Generally, you will need less roosters than hens, one rooster per 5 hens is a good ratio.

If you want to buy chicks, you must ensure they are well looked after and placed in a safe place. Chicks are more prone to developing diseases than chickens in their first 2 months of age, care should be taken that chicks are vaccinated against Marek's disease before buying them.

You should take care when transporting your pets to their new home. Whether you use a cardboard box, a cat carrier or a laundry basket, make sure that the box they are transported in does not allow much air to circulate through it. Violent air flow is detrimental for chicks.

Living with a Silkie chicken

Once you brought your new family members home, you must get into the habit of feeding them, cleaning their coop and looking after them properly. Soon they will get acclimated with their new home and they will explore the yard. Silkie chickens love hanging around and exploring their new surroundings.

Silkies are generally as easy to raise as other breeds of chickens but there are few differences and some extra care is needed.

It is important to give chickens free access to the backyard to dig for worms and feed on crawlies. They are adapted to outdoor life more than indoor life.

There is an increasing habit of raising silkies indoors. Some owners like to raise silkie chickens inside the house because they are furry like cats and dogs. But honestly, this is not as good an idea as it seems; first because chickens can poo everywhere and this is unpleasant, their droppings are wet and smelly. Second, droppings can carry pathogen bacteria like salmonella and E. Coli and health authorities prohibit raising chickens indoors. Third, silkies produce fluff and dust, their fluff may smell bad that you will want to get rid of it. Moreover, the dust can produce allergies in some people. So, it is recommended not to let them in the house and provide them with their own house.

Chickens are not perfect to be house pets like dogs or cats, but if you insist on keeping them in the house at your own risk, there are a few main things you should do: use chicken diapers so that they can move freely in the house without pooping everywhere, this may be a solution but finally this is not hygienic for the silkie vent, it may cause dropping to aggregate in their vent. It is recommended to provide them with their own private space and not let them roam the entire home or the kitchen.

Your next step is to give names for the new chickens. Names can be given based on their look or color. This book gives a good collection of chicken names that may help you to choose fancy chicken names. Look in name section in the final chapter.

Chapter 5. Feeding your silkie chickens

Chicken nutrition is undoubtedly the most important component in silkie chickens care. Chicken growth, welfare and health is largely related to the quality of the nutrition they receive. Good nutrition is the key to keeping your flock vivid and healthy.

A balanced diet is an important concept that any chicken caretaker should be familiar with. On big farms, the chicken's nutrition is well controlled, since every nutrient concentration is well calculated to meet the chicken's need, that's why nutritional deficiencies hardly happen. On the other hand, nutritional deficiencies occur mostly in backyard chickens, since some owners pay little or no attention to the chicken's feed.

Understanding chicken nutritional requirements as well as feeding best practices ensures your silkies live a long, happy life. In this chapter, nutritional requirements for silkie chickens as well as basic nutrition practices will be covered.

Food composition

Like humans, chickens are omnivorous. Their diet can be deduced from their wild ancestor's diet which is composed of insects, worms, fruits, seeds, leaves. To make sure your chickens stay healthy, their diet must be varied because vitamins and minerals have different concentrations in different food items.

Besides food, water is an essential element for the chicken, since it is involved in most chemical reactions in the body. Fresh and clean water should be provided daily. It is advisable to use a water supply system using nipples that keeps the water clean and always available.

Every feed is a mix of chemical compounds that have different roles in the body. In addition to water, feeds contain many chemical compounds that can be grouped into 5 main categories. Those categories are carbohydrates, proteins, fats, minerals and vitamins.

- Carbohydrates

Carbohydrates are big molecules of sugars. Their role is to furnish glucose, which is the fuel to all body cells. The brain only uses 50% of the body glucose to think, memorize and control movement. Muscle cells need glucose to perform contractions and produce movement.

Carbohydrates are essentially present in grains like wheat, corn and barley in the form of starch. The breakdown of starch in the intestines by an enzyme called amylase gives a smaller compound: the maltose which is a smaller carbohydrate that will be then converted into glucose.

- Proteins

Proteins are the building blocks of the body tissues, they are big chains of amino acids. Amino acids are required by the body to build his own proteins. Food proteins are essential to tissue growth and egg production.

Proteins are found in grains, insects and worms. High quality proteins are those that contain essential amino-acids. Essential amino-acids can't be synthetized and must come with food. Proteins are required at 20% in the diet of growing chicks.

- Fats

Fats are an important foodstuff. There are 2 types of fats: plant fats and animal fats. Their digestion produces fatty acids that are required for the body to produce energy and are involved many metabolic reactions. Essential oils are good for the feather quality.

- Minerals

Minerals are trace elements that are available in all food items. They are required to perform many chemical reactions and bones. Grains, fruits and vegetables contain minerals but in different concentrations. Important minerals are Calcium, Sodium, Magnesium, Potassium, Iron, Iodine, etc.

In rare cases, mineral deficiency occurs in backyard chickens. So, chickens should receive a supplement. Commercial feeds contain sufficient amounts of minerals.

- Vitamins

Vitamins are compounds that the body cannot synthetize and must be provided with food or synthetized in the caeca from precursors. Vitamins are different from proteins. They took their name from the combination of vital and amines, which are chemical groups that contain nitrogen in their structure.

There are two types of vitamins: lipophilic vitamins that come with fats and hydrophilic vitamins that can be dissolved in water. Some of the vitamins become oxidized. Chicken feeds are always added with preservatives to keep them stay active for a long period.

Keep in mind that the chicken diet should be supplemented with vitamin premix only if they are confined and don't have much area to eat grass and dig for worms.

The next table summarizes vitamin requirements for chickens. These values are for common breeds of chickens and they may be slightly different in silkie hens because they lay less often and therefore they require less vitamins. The table also shows some good sources of vitamins for people who feed raw diets.

Vitamins	Requirements per Kg of feed	Good sources
Vitamin A	Chickens: 1500 IU Hens: 4000 IU	Green grass, yellow corn, fish oils, green leaves, pigmented vegetables, liver, orange, carrots, potatoes, pumpkin, cantaloupe, abricots, synthetic carotene.
Vitamin D	Chickens: 200 IU Hens: 500 IU	Oily fish (Salmon, Tuna and sardines), oily seeds.
Vitamin E	Chickens: 10mg Hens: 5mg	Vegetable oils, green leafy vegetables, wheat germ, whole grains, avocados, tomatoes, watercress.
Vitamin K	Chickens: 0.5mg Hens: 0.5 mg	
Vitamin B1 (thiamin)	Chickens: 1.8 mg Hens: 0.8 mg	Cereals, whole grains, pasta, dried beans, soy foods

Vitamins	Requirements per Kg of feed	Good sources
Vitamin B2 (Riboflavin)	Chickens: 3.6 mg Hens: 2.2 mg	Yeasts, alfalfa meal, legumes, peas, lentils, asparagus.
Vitamin B6 (Pyridoxine)	Chickens: 3.5 mg Hens: 2.5 mg	Whole grains, potatoes, bananas, seeds, nuts, spinach.
Vitamin B5 (Pantothenic acid)	Chickens: 10 mg Hens: 2 mg	Widespread in foods, mushrooms, avocado, potatoes.
Vitamin B3 (Niacin)	Chickens: mg Hens: mg	Wheat products, peanuts
Vitamin B4 (Choline)	Chickens: 1300 mg Hens: 500 mg	Wheat soybean meal, fish, mushrooms.
Vitamin B7 (Biotin)	Chicks: 150µg Hens: 150µg	Yeasts, Alfalfa.
Vitamin B9 (Folic acid)	Chicks: 550µg Hens: 350µg	Liver, dried beans, green leafy vegetables, asparagus.
Vitamin B12 (Cobalamine)	Chicks: 9µg Hens: 3µg	Red meat, fish, broccoli, nuts and pulses, brown rice, whole grain cereals.

Source: the national research council of the United States

What to feed?

The easiest and most efficient way to feed a small flock of silkies is to purchase complete rations that are available in feed stores like mashes, pellets or crumbles. These feeds are complete and balanced. They provide all the nutrients required for your chickens without having to worry about nutritional deficiencies.

With home-made diets, chickens it is unclear if their diet is balanced or not. But this may be later reflected on their health and look. It is recommended that their diet should be varied with unrestricted access to the garden grass, they may be able to eat grass and worms and satisfy their nutritional requirements.

It is recommended that chicks start out with starter feed and avoid medicated feed unless they have any history of illnesses. The starter feed has a high protein content of 20%. If chicks are with their mother, they will eat their mother's diet if the feeders are on the floor. It is recommended to provide the chicks with feeders containing their starter feed and hang the hens' feeders to make them not reachable for chicks. When chicks reach 6 weeks old, then switch to the grower feed.

Grower feed contains a protein content of 16%. This feed should be continued until chicks reach 4 to 5 months. Then switch to the layer formula.

It is advisable to feed your adult laying hens feed. Regular layer feed has a higher Calcium content that is necessary for laying hens to build the egg shell. Avoid the broiler feed because they do not require the amount of proteins a broiler needs.

The amount of complete feed consumed may be reducedby supplementing with pasture. Green grass provides valuable nutrients and fresh vitamins for chickens as well as meal worms.

Shell grit is also important in the chickens' diet if chickens don't have access to the garden or when the garden doesn't have enough grit. It has 2 roles: it helps in crushing the feed in the gizzard and it is a rich source of Calcium that helps your hens form the egg shell.

For layer hens, egg production is a demanding task. It requires nutrients to build a good nutritive egg. Therefore, hens must receive good nutrition to lay eggs in excellent quality.

Pet chickens shouldn't be fed a diet of dog or cat food. This pet food composition is not suitable for chickens because they are high in protein and fat. For chickens, there are mainly 2 types of feed options available for: commercial feeds and homemade diets.

- Commercial feeds

Commercial feeds come in many varieties and target specific stages of life and types of chickens. For every life stage of a chicken, there are commercial feeds that fit their needs. So, a chick starter mash is completely different than adult chicken feed. And there are plenty of chicken feeds that target each type of chicken.

There are many types of adult chicken feeds. There is a feed for layer hens. There are feeds for broilers and there are feeds for dual-purpose breeds. The major difference between these types of feeds is dictated by the nutritional requirements of each category of chickens as well as their feeding behavior.

A commercial feed for laying hens is nutritionally balanced and has the proper ratios of minerals and vitamins for a proper egg production. Laying hens require higher amounts of Calcium to build egg shells. You don't have to worry about balancing the diet and adding supplements with this feed.

Newly hatched chicks need a feed with a higher percentage of proteins as they are growing. Chick starter feed contains between 20-24% proteins. The chicken feed needs to be presented in small particles that can be easily picked and swallowed.

There are also medicated feeds for chicks, which contain anticoccidial drugs to prevent coccidiosis in chicks, these are only recommended if you have problems of coccidia in your flock.

Commercial feeds often contain synthetic vitamins which can be quickly oxidized. It is important to store chicken feed in a dry place with no light exposure that may alter the feed quality.

There are also chicken treats that are rich in protein like dried mealworms. Dried mealworms are delicious and help chickens in molting periods to grow feathers. Some chicken keepers grow worms in the garden and they give them to their chickens.

Commercial feeds are designed to meet chicken requirements and are recommended if you don't have enough yard space for chickens to dig the ground and eat grit. Mineral and vitamin supplements are necessary only if the diet is imbalanced. That's when you are feeding your chickens on limited options like seeds or grains.

For show silkies, a supplement with omega 3 fatty acids is good for the quality of their feathers. It makes them have much prettier and shiny feathers. Probiotics are also good nutritional additives that can be added to boost the gut flora.

- Homemade diets

Homemade diets are also popular among chicken keepers. They can be whole or cracked grains, seeds and scraps, scratch grains, treats and fresh mealworms, meat scraps, pasta, vegetation, worms, insects, grit, etc. Homemade diets have the advantage of being fresh and providing fresh vitamins and amino acids. But sometimes, they are not balanced.

Backyards are not often rich in grit and minerals, so chickens fed these types of diets are more prone to nutritional deficiencies. This problem can be overcome by varying the feeds you give to your chickens to avoid getting into nutritional imbalances and deficiencies.

It essential to feed your chickens a balanced diet; either you feed them commercial feed or homemade mixture.

How much to feed?

The answer to this is to give her enough food until she stops eating. There are 2 types of feeding regimens for pet chickens: a free regimen and a time-controlled regimen.

- Free feeding regimen

In this regimen, feeders are filled with commercial feed and chickens can eat at any time they want. Feeders are only filled when the food level becomes low. Like that, chickens have access to feed at all day times. This is the most used regimen among chicken keepers. It has the advantage of minimizing competition about food and preventing dominance. All chickens get the amount of food they want since the feed is always abundant. The drawback of this regimen is that feed kept for a long time in the feeder attracts pests and especially rodents. There will be some feed lost due to rodents, unless you control pests in the coop. In addition, feed nutrients may partially lose their nutritional quality and freshness as they are more susceptible to be oxidized.

- Time-controlled feeding regimen

As its name suggests, feed is distributed in fixed daytimes; in the morning and in the evening. The amount of food should be well estimated to make sure all chickens eat a sufficient amount of food. This regimen has the advantage of avoiding feed spoilage in the coop and food is always fresh but this method makes chickens way more aggressive and fight for food it promotes dominance in the flock.

Regardless of the feeding method you will adopt, you must ensure all chickens are well fed and satisfied. If you are adopting the first feeding regimen, you don't have to worry about how much to feed, since silkies eat the amount of feed they need. If you distribute the food at different times, then make sure all the chickens have received their meal.

A mature bantam silkie chicken consumes an average of 2.5oz per day, so manage 1.2oz for each chicken in one meal. In addition to the commercial feed, it is an excellent idea to give silkies fresh scarps of fruit and vegetables whenever possible and give them unrestricted access to the yard grass. Chickens love grass and it is a rich source of fresh vitamins and minerals. Silkies love to fetch small gravels to help them digest food.

Water supply

Water is vital to chickens and it must be available at all times. It is essential for body development and is involved in most of chemical reactions in the body. A young chicks body contains more than 80% water. A grown chickens body contains around 70%. The egg is 65% composed of water.

The volume of water consumed by chickens is 1.5 times the volume of food she consumes in a day. Water deprivation for half a day has an adverse effect on growth of young chicks and egg production of hens.

The volume of water drank by chickens may vary. Many factors influence the volume of water that chickens drink like the environmental temperature, relative humidity, salt and protein levels of the diet.

Chapter 6. Silkie chicken care and grooming

Now that you are responsible for your silkies welfare, you naturally want to give your furry family members the best possible care. First let's start with the daily routine.

Collecting and storing eggs

Eggs are your silkie's reward for caring for them. Silkies don't lay eggs daily but if your chicken's brood contains many hens, then you may get enough eggs. Eggs stay fresh in the chicken nest for 3 days. Collecting eggs is generally done in the morning since hens lay in the early morning.

The eggs must be stored in a dry, clean place. They must not be washed, as this may make egg germs penetrate the eggs through the shell holes. The eggs can be stored at room temperature or in the fridge. Only store eggs in the fridge if they will be consumed.

Refrigerated storage is necessary if you want to keep eggs edible for a longer period that may last up to 4 weeks. The eggs that you will incubate must be stored at a room temperature. Fertilized eggs need some air circulation so that they can breathe.

Eggs can last for quite a long time and remain able to hatch. This period must not exceed 10 days. Longer period of storage may not give hatchable eggs because the fertility dramatically drops.

Cleaning the coop

The coop should always be clean and well organized, this is to ensure the chickens are in good health as well as to avoid any unpleasant odor that may be released from it. The odors from the litter may cause neighbors to be angry. So, it is important to keep the coop always clean as well as keeping chickens under control while roaming in the garden.

Coop cleaning should be done on a regular basis. You should assess the bedding every time and change the litter whenever needed. Fresh chicken droppings produce odors and attract flies and insects. A thick bedding should be used to provide a soft and dry surface for chickens and to absorb dropping moisture and help in odor control.

This also helps to protect chicken legs and keep them dry. Poor bedding or lack of cleaning can be easily deduced from examining chicken legs. So, it is important to change the bedding once a week. Depending on the size and the area of the chicken coop, chicken litter must be changed regularly.

Many people just toss the new clean bedding on top of the old rather than cleaning the old bedding out. This may provide insulation and therefore warmth, but it is not hygienic for silkie's legs and will attract bugs and germs. The odors also get smellier and ammonia levels raise to alarming levels that may cause respiratory problems for chickens.

The litter should be thick enough to protect chickens' legs from the rigid floor. There are many materials used as beddings. The most common beddings used are wood shavings, paper products, wood chips, sand, hay and rice hulls.

Wood shavings are the best products to be used because they absorb moisture. If not available, you can use straw or sand but change them more frequently to avoid litter impaction. Generally, it is recommended to manage a thickness of 1 or 2 inches of wood shavings or 2 inches of hay. If the bedding gets wet fast, then think of changing the litter more often or make it thicker. If the chickens have free access to the garden, their droppings will have to be drought faster and scattered on the yard.

Waste litter should be stored in plastic bags to be used as compost. Chicken droppings are considered strong manure. It is rich in nitrogen and serves for soils low in nitrogen or for some type of plants like grapes. It contains higher amounts of phosphorus and potassium than another animals' manure. It can be used as an excellent organic fertilizer. So, don't throw it and rather keep it for use in the garden.

Over time, the chicken coop may develop an unpleasant aroma. A dirty coop can cause health problems because of bacteria built-up and shedding bugs and parasites. So, you may need to clean the floor with water and detergent. It is extremely helpful to reduce bugs and odors.

To kill bugs and parasites, use lime powder or a mixture of diluted bleach and water with a 1:30 ratio of bleach to water to wash the surfaces. After that, keep the coop empty for a day or two to completely dry it out.

Neutralizing chicken coop odor takes time and effort. But it is crucial to the health of your flock.

Feather Grooming

Silkie chickens need some grooming to make sure their feathers stay beautiful and clean. You must deal with their fluffy feathers. Bearded silkie chickens require some grooming since their feathers need extra care.

Their head feathers can pose a problem if they cover their eyes and make them unable to see. If you don't pay attention to that, silkies will bump into objects and sometimes get injured. Plus, they cannot see their food and water and therefore don't eat. So, it is important to trim back face feathers or tie them up using a headband.

You will know if your bird needs a little feather trimming by holding him at your eye level. If you can see the eyes, then nothing is needed. If not, plucking or trimming is necessary for the chicken to see the wonderful world again. But the question here is what is better; to trim or to pluck off feathers? That depends on your intention, to show the silkie chicken or not.

If you will show the chicken, then you should pluck the feathers. Plucked feathers can grow back in few weeks. You must do it gently and try not to hurt the chicken.

Plucking needs to be done regularly, every 6 weeks. The feathers that are above and below the eyes and those in front of the eye should be plucked gently. Try to do it symmetrically on both face sides, check by holding the bird at eye level and look for the bird's eyes to see if he has a lot of space to see. Crest feathers can be pinned back using a hair tie. This allows the chickens to see well and gives him a cute look.

The chicken eyes need care since he is always getting hit on them. The eyes can get infected because the face feathers constantly irritate them. So, after trimming the feathers, check if the eyes are swollen or have discharge. Use an eye ointment that contains antibiotics. Contact your vet to get the correct ointment. This helps relieve the eye damage and help your chicken to see normally again.

Leg feathers are quite a nice feature. But this makes them closer to the wet bedding and droppings stick to these feathers and with time they may cause toe infections or their toes may become a compacted ball of solid droppings. This usually happens when there is lack of cleaning the litter.

If their legs are becoming dirty, you may need to brush their legs with warm water and shampoo using a toothbrush to clean them. Replace the litter and keep it clean and dry to preserve the legs from dirt.

The fluffy butt can sometimes hold onto bits of poop. In this case, trimming the vent feathers can reduce the dirt.

Dyeing Silkies

Have you ever seen silkies with very unusual colors? There are silkies that come in fancy colors, like pink or light blue, red, and yellow. These silkies have been colored using food colorings.

Dyed silkie chickens are for fun purposes and are not allowed in shows since they do not meet the show standards. Dyeing silkies is a relatively safe procedure that anyone can do at home. All you need is a food coloring and a tooth brush or a spray and here is how you can do it:

- Coloring silkie chickens:

If you want to make your chicken's feathers look fancy, use a food coloring solution. Dyeing works best on white-feathered chickens. Find some edible food dye that is sold in your local grocery store. These are vegetable-based food colors in many colors: blue, red, green and yellow.

You will need to dye your chickens in the cellar or in a safe place where you can do this. You may need a helper to hold the chicken and keep it calm while you are performing your artwork. You should prepare your coloring bowls. So, pour a few drops of each color into its own small bowl.

You can perform dyeing using a toothbrush, or you can do it using a little spray that you fill with food coloring. First, bathe the silkie to clean its feathers. Use a little shampoo and foam it gently. Then rinse it. Use the toothbrush to color the feathers. Dip it into the food coloring and use it to gently rub the dye onto the chickens' feathers.

Try to cover all the chicken's feathers and be careful to avoid the chicken's eyes and orifices. You can use more than one color per chicken to get a rainbow silkie. Allow the dye to dry using a hair dryer. Now you have a dyed silkie.

With time, the food coloring gradually fades from the feathers or it may be replaced with new feathers as the chicken molts. This can take some time, so don't use dye if you intend to show or sell your chickens soon.

- Dyeing Chicken Embryos

Dyeing embryos is quite a delicate procedure and you should not do it alone the first time. You can kill the embryo by a false maneuver or by dyeing at the wrong time. So, these methods are cited for your own knowledge. Embryo dyeing will produce dyed chicks at hatching. So, it's possible to inject dye into chicken eggs during the incubation period. This process is tough and completely safe if done correctly.

The safest time to inject the chicken embryos with dye is between the 11th and 14th day of incubation, though it can be done as early as the 10th or as late as the 19th. All you need is a 2 or 3% solution of the vegetable-based dye. Any color can be used to dye the embryos, especially on naturally white chickens. Blue, green and red tend to work best. You will also need a hypodermic syringe with a needle, 95% alcohol solution and molted paraffin. To do this, you must dye the incubated eggs in order and one by one. Try to do this as quickly as possible to preserve the eggs.

Gather all the tools. Fill the syringe with the dyeing solution to inject it inside the egg. Injection should be done one-half an inch from the small end of the egg just below the inner shell membrane. It should be done slowly and carefully to avoid overflowing and to prevent it from harming the embryo. After you have removed the needle, cover up the hole with a drop of melted paraffin wax to protect the embryo from infection. Then rub the small ends with a 95% alcohol solution to disinfect them. Return the eggs to the incubator, where they should continue to incubate as normal. Try to avoid any false maneuver or cracking the egg, otherwise, you will kill your chicks.

Controlling pests

The chicken coop is a warm place with food and water. This may attract some uninvited guests. You may face some new intruders to your new chickens' home. Rodents are a major source of disturbance for chickens and controlling rodents should not be neglected.

Mice and rats are the most encountered pests. They are omnivorous and nocturnal. They are attracted by the chicken feed and they infiltrate the coop to steal it. They can also eat eggs and even young chicks.

Rodents are nocturnal and most active from nightfall till dawn. They hide in the day and prowl around their environment at night looking for food. The coop should not contain any place for rodents to hide. If the floor is not cemented, then rodents can burrow the litter and inhabit the coop. They can soon multiply, as they reproduce fast. So, it is better to prevent pests than dealing with a present population of them.

All that rodents want is food and chicken feed is their target. So, try to store chicken feed in a safe and enclosed place. Feed should not be stored in the coop. Besides rodents, insects can also infiltrate the feed bag and alter the nutritive value of the feed. Try to keep the feeding area clean and dry and try to minimize the waste of food in the litter.

If you already have a pest infestation in your garden, then you should change to defensive methods. There are many ways to control mice or rats like chemical rodenticides or traps. If you are using mousetraps, try to put traps outside the coop to avoid trapping your silkies.

There are many models of traps you can find on the market. Poison bait are more mass destructive. Remember to place the bait where children, pets and curious silkies can't get to it. It is better to inform children about the bait so they stay informed and nothing bad happens.

Rodents are intelligent enough to escape some control measures. In fact, with time, rats and mice can understand that these measures are fatal and learn to escape them. A clever idea consists of consistently changing the control measure. Change the tactics every time to get better results.

There are some devices that keep rodents away. These devices emit a deterrent light that scares nocturnal pest animals and many of them are solar powered. These devices are effective and can be used to keep the coop safe at night.

You have to keep the feed safe from moths, weevils and meal worms, too. They attack stored feed and lower the quality of the feed. Even though many people use pesticides, rats and mice may still remain in small numbers.

The coop can sometimes host other insects that feed on the litter and that may cause a nuisance for chickens. Flies are attracted by moist litter and food particles. They are generally harmless for chickens but can transmit diseases. Use spray insecticides to keep them away.

Vaccination

There is a lot of debate about backyard chickens' vaccination. Some people are for, others are against. Above all, vaccination is an important prevention tool against most threatening chicken diseases. It is a prevention tool and not a cure.

Vaccines are just an amazing discovery in medicine and their use is important in chickens and many other pets. Vaccines are killed or deactivated pathogens that stimulate the immune system. The body develops antibodies against that pathogen. The immune system then keeps track of that pathogen and when there is an infection with this pathogen, a quicker immune response is fired to stop it from multiplying and harming the body.

Vaccines should be given only to healthy birds. Vaccination is stressful and can't be given to sick birds because they cannot withstand the stress of vaccination.

Chicken epidemics happen rarely. But when they happen, their effects are massive. It is better getting them vaccinated against major threatening diseases. Vaccination is not common among backyard chicken keepers. Vaccination becomes necessary only if the flock have had disease problems in the past.

If you are raising show silkies, you must get them vaccinated since they are exposed to other chickens and diseases can spread fast.

Chickens are generally vaccinated against diseases that are present in the surrounding regions. You can speak to your vet to ask about frequent diseases and if you should vaccinate your flock. Refer to your local vet to get the list of vaccines and their due times. Marek's disease is a widespread disease and has long destroyed lots of backyard chickens and vaccination of chicks is strongly recommended.

Chicks should be purchased already vaccinated against Marek's disease, either in the hatchery at one-day old or while incubation. Silkie chicks that are purchased from local farms or neighbours should be vaccinated at their first day of age. Contact your vet to get them vaccinated.

Vaccination schedules are variable and depend on the area and existing diseases. Vaccines that are available for commercial poultry are rarely used in backyard poultry, first because most vaccines are concentrated and are intended for large flocks. Second, some of them are injected subcutaneously and are not available for sale for small flocks.

Some veterinarians perform vaccinations of individual birds. A description of the common vaccines is presented here to get a reference.

- Marek's Disease: 1-day old or while incubation.
- Infectious bursal disease: 2 weeks old.
- Infectious Bronchitis: 3 weeks, 5 weeks and 8 weeks old.
- Newcastle disease: 3 weeks, 5 weeks and 8 weeks old.
- Fowl pox: 12 weeks old.
- Encephalomyelitis: 12 weeks old.
- Mycoplasma gallisepticum: 14 weeks old.

The program is used in big laying hen houses where the security of the flock is critical. Many vaccinations are used to make sure the hens receive the maximum protection. Backyard chickens are quite resistant to diseases, only Marek's vaccine and Newcastle vaccine are commonly used. Fowl pox vaccine may be necessary if there has been a history of pox disease in the pen.

Deworming

Deworming is administering drugs to control intestinal worms. Chickens usually have a healthy level of parasites within them that helps boost their immunity and make them stronger.

Worm infestation is common and sometimes it can have damaging effects on chickens and many owners are not aware of that. Worms colonize the gut and lungs and may grow, causing serious gut problems and even be fatal for chickens.

Worms live inside chickens' guts and lungs and in their environment. They reproduce inside chickens and infect new chicks at an early age. Most common worms are Gape worms and gut worms.

Chickens get worms from the environment. Hosting worms may not be harmful in most cases. Gut worms feed on the gut chyme and lay eggs that are excreted with feces. In younger chicks, this will cause malnutrition and gut obstruction.

There are many reports from veterinarians of chicken deaths caused by intestinal impaction and obstruction with worms. So, it is recommended to treat chickens regularly. Silkie chickens, as well as many other bantam chicken breeds, are very susceptible to worms.

There are plenty of drugs to treat worms. Each drug is active against a group of worm species. Famous active molecules are Fenbendazole, Levamisole, Pyrantel and Piperazine. There are also natural deworming agents that are sold alone or in medicated feeds. Apple Cider Vinegar and pumpkin seeds are famous natural deworming agents and are effective against gut parasites.

Deworming should be done regularly; once every month for chicks and once every 3 months for adult chickens. Refer to your vet to get the correct drugs, dosages and how to use them.

Handling and transporting your chickens

Being cute pets, silkies are always picked up and cuddled by kids and friends. They soon get used to human manipulation. You will need to handle chickens to cuddle them, to examine them or to move them.

Handling can be delicate only if you are new to silkie raising. You need to know how to handle your chickens to inspect their feathers or to do some grooming. Sometimes accidents occur when trying to handle a chicken. A chicken doesn't know your intentions every time you pick her up. Sometimes she thinks that you intend to harm her. She may squawk and shake her wings violently trying to escape.

Silkies are more docile than many other breeds of chickens. But caution should always be taken when dealing with them and especially the chicks.

Here we are going to cover how to safely handle your chickens and reduce the stress that might be caused by improper manipulations.

First thing's first, if you have recently introduced new chickens to the coop, don't handle them unless there is a real need for that. Chickens get stressed when they are picked off the ground, especially when the chicken is new to the coop. To catch a silkie, you should do this when the flock is at rest in the night or when they are eating in the coop. It is much easier done in the night with a flashlight. Nevertheless, they can be caught easily in the day because they are easy-going and do not resist to handling as other chicken breeds do. The best way to catch a chicken is isolating all the flock in a small area in the coop to avoid chasing and running after them.

Chasing chickens is stressful, they run fast and you may take much unnecessary time doing this. With time, silkies will get used to you and then all you'll need is to call them and they come to your feet. To grab a silkie, hold both hands around them and pick them up with both hands. Hold their wings to their bodies so they don't flap their wings and try to escape. Don't grab them from the neck or by the legs. They may react and move their legs and involuntarily make bad movements that may break the legs or damage the joints.

To catch a chick, put one hand in front of him and try with the other hand to sweep him onto it. Hold the chick with one hand and make his head pop between two fingers. Don't grab a chick by its legs as they are so vulnerable. Don't squeeze the chick in your hand. If you cover the chick eyes, he may become calmer. Don't hold him for long, free him after you're done with your examination.

You may need to transport your chicken from one place to another or from a store to your backyard or when you take one of them to the vet. Transporting chickens is delicate, since chickend get very stressed when transported.

It is important to manage a small cage of transportation for chickens. A cat cage is suitable for transporting chickens. If not available, then a cardboard box can do the job. Remember to create small holes of half inch in diameter in the box to let the air inside the box.

Make sure that the transportation bow is wide enough and not too tight for the chicken. The box should be closed since the chicken can move and try to escape. The darker the box is, the calmer the chicken will be. Some people tie the legs together to minimize movements, this can be done and the strap should be not tight.

Taming silkies

Many people get excited when they see videos or shows of silkie chickens that perform some tricks like jumping on their owner's knee or eating from the hand. Like all other pets, chickens can be motivated to do some tricks by gaining their trust and rewarding them.

Handling them and earning their trust is the key to taming. Some silkies will be more outgoing than others. Chickens are not as smart as dogs or cats and taming may not give good results, but it is worth a try.

Handling baby chicks frequently makes them tamer when they're older. To succeed in your taming, you should feed them at fixed times each day so they will give you more interest and they know that you are their feeder, chickens recognize their caretaker and remember people who scare them.

Once your silkies get used to you and you earn their trust, they will get closer to you and eat from your hand. Some hens may not seem good at taming and sometimes you get deceiving results. But taming needs time and patience to give good results.

Chapter 7. Breeding silkie chickens

Silkie chicken breeding is an easy task. Minimal human intervention is needed to control it. Their strong broodiness instinct makes reproduction a prioritized issue.

Choosing good breeders

When intending to expand your flock, you should look for good hens and a good rooster. You should select your breeders based on their morphological traits and check for their drawbacks. Discard chickens with a big skull vault to avoid getting chicks with wryneck.

The number of silkie males must be less that females. The ratio should be theoretically no less than 1 male for every 8 hens, but since silkies have a calm temperament, you can even lower the ratio to one rooster per 5 hens. If the rooster is active, then most of the eggs you collect from your coop are fertile. But this does not mean that their taste will be any different from unfertilized ones! They are both edible and most of us have eaten many fertile eggs for years.

When a hen is inseminated, her future eggs will be fertilized for up to 3 weeks. This is because the sperm stays active for about 3 weeks in her oviduct stored in sperm host glands or "sperm nests" scattered along the hen's oviduct. The sperm is continuously released, making future ova fertile for many days. So, you don't have to be anxious if the rooster is not mating with hens daily.

Regardless of the environment where eggs are incubated, commercial hatcheries or in your local coop nests, not all the incubated eggs will hatch.

The percentage of hatched eggs or hatchability is not always 100%. It depends on many factors including the egg fertilization, its nutritional composition, incubation parameters as well as some diseases that can kill the embryo which can be transmitted from mothers during egg formation.

What if eggs are unfertilized?

If you keep hens with no rooster, then you don't have to wait for chicks. But hens repeatedly go broody. If eggs are unfertilized or you don't want to incubate eggs, you must remove these eggs and try to get the hen back to its normal life. You must collect eggs daily and move the hen to the rest of the flock. Give her treats to distract her and close the nest. If all this doesn't succeed, then separate the hen from the rest of the flock for a while. Put her in a cage to initiate the change in hormone secretion. This may help her break her broodiness.

Sometimes, many hens may crowd into a single nest box at one time. This is because they are all broody. They compete for one nest. If the number of eggs is limited, you don't have to use more than one hen to incubate the eggs. The other hens should get back to their normal life. Tips on breaking broodiness will be explained later.

Egg formation

It is amazing how birds start their life inside eggs. A chicken embryo develops outside the mother's body. It develops fast and it only takes 21 days for a fertilized egg to make a chick.

As you know, the egg is composed of 3 compartments: the white, the yolk, and an air chamber. These compartments are separated by thin membranes. The yellow part of an unfertilized egg contains the egg cell or the ovum, which will create the embryo if it is fertilized by a spermatozoid.

The egg cell can sometimes be visible to the naked eye on the egg yellow surface. When the egg is fertilized, the embryo begins its development process inside the hen oviduct and feeds on the yellow. Once the mother hen lays the egg, the embryo development stops temporarily until incubation takes place.

You cannot tell whether an egg is fertile or not from the shell. To relieve your curiosity, you can crack some eggs and see. Embryo cells, or blastoderm, can be simply detected on the yellow if you are an egg cracking expert. The blastoderm of the fertile egg looks like a white spot surrounded by a white halo. It looks like an eyeball as many people love to say. This trick is not the best choice to do when you intend to hatch eggs. This is meant only to say "Oh, this one was actually fertilized"!

How to know if an egg is fertilized without cracking it? It is just simple; incubation and time will tell. Simply incubate them with a broody silkie or put them in the hatcher, and then, using a special technique called egg candling you can know for sure whether there is an embryo or not.

In nature, the percentage of fertile eggs is high when the rooster is in good shape and chickens are often seen after mating. Most of the eggs, if not all, are fertile if you have a good mature rooster. You often get good results with a rooster above one-year old because its sperm is of good quality.

Egg incubation

Egg formation takes an average of 24 or 25 hours. It passes through many steps to get finally laid. Due to their frequent broodiness, egg-laying is often interrupted. So, if you have a broody hen and you intend to have new baby chicks, collect all the eggs daily and store them in a dry place at room temperature.

If you reach a good number of eggs laid in the last 7 days, place them all in the nest of the broody hen. This step must be done once because future chicks must hatch together. You can put eggs 1 day or 2 after incubation begins, they hatch successfully. Ideally, eggs should not be more than 7 days old when they are set.

Like other chickens, Silkies take 21 days to hatch. If you incubate them in a hatcher, wait one or two extra days. There are some reports about delay in embryo development when incubation parameters change.

A broody hen is a biologic incubator for eggs. Temperature and humidity are good for embryos to develop. The temperature of incubation is 102°F with a humidity of 80%. Broody hens often move eggs many times a day to keep embryos alive.

If an artificial incubator is used, care must be taken to ensure all the parameters are perfect. Incubators are usually equipped with an automatic rotator for eggs and proper ventilation. Some incubators require manual moving of the eggs. But with silkie chickens, you don't have to use an artificial incubator. They can do the job well.

Many people still prefer to use the incubator. There are plenty of makes and models of egg incubators with varied egg capacity and of course they vary in price. There are even Styrofoam types found at most feed stores, they hold many more eggs and are usually less expensive.

When placed in the incubator, eggs should be set in a normal position as it would on a flat surface or upright in egg turners with the round end of the egg always up. An egg that has the small edge up may cause the embryo to be disoriented with the head toward the small edge. Like that, the chick is likely to die. Turning the eggs is essential in incubation. If it is done by hand, turn the eggs an uneven number of times a day so that eggs does not spent two nights in the same position. If not, the embryo touches the shell and sticks to it, having an abnormal growth. Turning the egg keeps an embryo centered in the egg and mimics what a mother hen would do naturally.

Assessing embryos viability

If all of your eggs have hatched, that's a good sign of the good health of the flock. Often, some eggs don't hatch. First because there may be an embryo mortality or some unfertilized eggs or there may be an embryo infection from mother hens. The percent hatchability in the commercial poultry industry ranges from 78 to 88%.

You don't need to wait for dead embryos to hatch. You would better eliminate them to spare effort for the setting hen or free some space if you are using an incubator. Embryo vitality can be assessed using an egg candler, which is a simple device with a lamp that helps see an image of the embryo development. You can make your own candler using basic tools that you can stick together to form a candler. Or simply buy it!

In fact, in the old days it used to be done with the flame from a candle. The main requirement is a bright light with an opening smaller than the diameter of the eggs. Candling is better done in a dark room or in dimly light room. It is performed simply by placing the round end of the egg at the tip of the candle and looking at the inside of the egg.

An unfertilized egg will appear as a bright egg with no blood vessels while a dead embryo will look like a small dark halo inside the egg. Viable embryos will show red blood vessels. After 21 days, one day less or more, you can observe chicks hatching out of their eggs, pecking at the eggshell using the egg-tooth. It is advisable not to help them while they are hatching because this can cause them to bleed. Hatching may take few hours. When the chicks get out of the egg, they are wet and loudly chirping.

Generally, silkie egg incubation gives good rates. Most of the time all the eggs hatch and you get new fluffy friends. In some cases, a small proportion of the eggs hatch. Some diseases can reduce the fertility of the flock. It is hard to know the real cause of why egg hatchability is low.

Brooding chickens

Brooding is the period from hatching until supplemental heat is no longer needed. The management of chicks is a bit delicate and requires commitment and attention. Silkie chicks are vulnerable and require a warm environment since their body's thermoregulation is not effective.

Hens do pretty well at brooding chicks, no care is needed with hens, but if you have orphan chicks or you used a hatcher to breed the chicks, then you will do the job yourself. Chicks should be raised inside boxes with a heating bulb, feeders and drinkers.

The area in which chicks will be placed should be set-up prior to thechickens' arrival to ensure the bedding has warmed up to the brooding temperature so that the chicks don't get cold. The brooding area should provide food and water to ensure a good start for the silkie chicks.

The brooding layout should be circular with a heating bulb in the center. Feed and water should be alternatively placed around the bulb to make it evenly distributed to all chicks. The use of thermometers is indispensable in the brooding area.

The key here is to place the heating bulb above the brooding area at the height that permits the litter to warm up to this temperature. This procedure must be done a few hours before the introduction of chicks to the area.

It is critical to observe the chicks in the first hour and assess their behavior. It is completely normal that one-day-old chicks don't seem so interested in food because they still have some remaining vitellus in their abdomen that keeps them nurtured for up to 2 days. Some of them will try to peck the litter or the food.

The temperature should be homogenously distributed in the brooding area. If so, chicks should be homogenously scattered in the area like shown in the following figure. If the temperature is higher than needed, chicks tend to be placed alongside the perimeter of the enclosure. That means that the lamp should be lifted a little higher to reduce the heat of the area beneath it. If chicks seem aggregated below the heat bulb and noisy chirping occurs, this indicates that they are cold. The lamp should be lowered. Normally this procedure should be done prior to chicks' arrival.

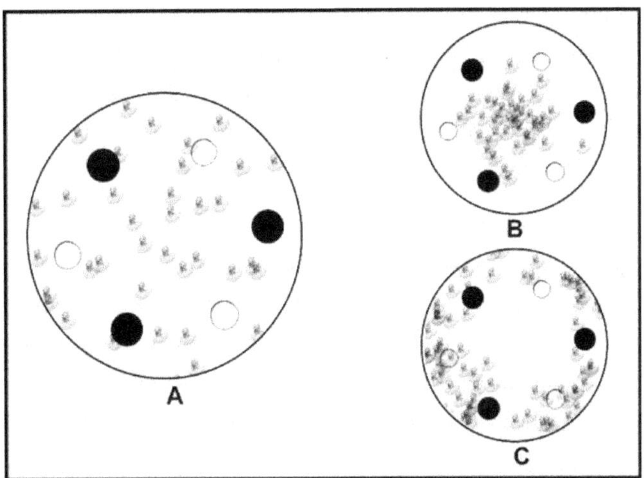

A: heat is well distributed, B: lack of heat, C: excess of heat

The temperature should normally be 95°F for the first week, then it must be decreased by 5∘F each week until the outdoor temperature is met. The chicks should live in the new box for about 6 weeks until they have lots of strong feathers and can handle cooler temperatures. The chicks should then be moved to their new home in the coop.

Depending on the outside temperature, this may be delayed until spring when it will be warmer for them. In the coop, the silkie chicks grow and grow and reach adult size at about 3-4 months. Along the way, they get tons of new feathers and will shed their old ones, as well as leave a lot of bird dander all over the place.

Silkie chicks should be fed grower feed for 6 weeks old until they reach 4 or 5 months. This guarantees their optimal growth and makes them ready for puberty.

Chicks should be protected and handled as gently as possible because they are more vulnerable to head accidents. As the chick grows, the bones in the vaulted area usually close together and the risk of brain injury drops. It is good practice to separate silkie chicks with big vaulted skulls into a separate brooder for their safety.

How to distinguish male chicks from females?

The normal percentage rate of gender distribution is about 50% roosters and 50% pullets. In reality, there are lots of variations. It is good to know the gender of young silkies to give them names and better identify them. It may be hard to tell whether chicks are male or female until they grow up and the sexual dimorphism becomes easy to figure out.

In adult chickens, males can be easier distinguished from females. Sometimes, silkie pullets take too long to start laying. Well, if it is not a falsely labeled male, laying delay is due to many factors including the genetic potential, the environment and the nutrition. If the pullet is known to have good parents, then there are some diseases that can delay and reduce laying. Some of the important diseases will be cited for information in the dedicated chapter.

In chicks, determining the gender can be hard and less accurate. Knowing the gender is a matter of time. It may be a little hard for non-experienced people to do it. You can get familiar with it after you do more sexing exercises. It is easier done in elderly chickens; females are self-indicating after they start laying eggs and males start crowing. Their first crowings are timid and are not loud. With time, they will train themselves to make it perfect, this may be as early as 4 months or more. There are more other morphological hints that you can rely on a little earlier to tell who are boys and who are girls.

✓ Comb and wattles

Regardless of the gender, wattles are more enlarged in non-bearded silkies than in bearded ones. Bearded silkies have a big beard under the beak and that makes the wattles unseen. Non-bearded silkie chicks start to grow wattles earlier than bearded silkies. But within the same variety.

Roosters usually develop a comb and wattles a bit earlier than hens do. Observing chicks of the same litter over a period after they reach 2 months old can help in determining their gender if you note the differences; the males will show wattles and the females won't yet. The comb and wattles are larger in males than in females and remain a distinctive mark for males.

✓ Overall look

Male chickens grow faster than females. If they are at the same age, males are taller than females with a bigger body size and with a more upright posture than females. The size must be taken into consideration only if the chicks have the same age. Size may not be the most accurate tool if the ages are different.

There are some other hints that you can rely on to determine the sex. Experienced silkie owners rely on the streamers to identify males. The streamers are special feathers that can be noticed in males. A female has a rounded crest.

The male will have some longer feathers that stream backward from the lower part of the crest called streamers. The streamers will begin to develop between the ages of 4 to 5 months after their juvenile molting. These streamers are hard to figure out for beginners. Furthermore, not all male silkies develop streamers. In some silkies, streamers are quite obvious and they can tell that this is definitely a rooster.

✓ Vent Sexing

Vent sexing is an early sexing method that can be used in all breeds of chickens, including silkies. It requires delicate handling and experience. This method involves applying a gentle pressure on the vent to invert it and examine the cloaca for male sex organs.

This method is adapted in commercial hatcheries with experienced workers to identify future pullets and raise them separately. Highly skilled workers have around a 95 percent accuracy. But amateurs are usually no more successful than 60 to 70 percent.

To get an accurate sexing, you must contact an avian vet. But this method is not a major breakthrough, it is recommended to avoid it because you may harm the chick's vent.

✓ The wing method

You may hear of some owners that are able to do feather sexing in newly hatched chicks. This method can only be accomplished in some breeds of chickens at the age of 1 or 2 days. But no studies or experiences on silkie chickens support it. This method is based on observing the difference in wing featherings; primaries are smaller in the pullet and have the same length as the coverts. Silkies can't be sexed using this method because this trait is related to a specific gene, which is only carried by some specific breeds and even certain strains of those breeds are specifically selected for that.

Chapter 8. Showing your silkies

Silkie chickens are popular in shows. To master silkie chickens' shows, it advisable to attend shows and ask breeders to get good ideas. Once you get the minimal skills, you can start your show business.

Qualification of show silkies depends on a set of criteria that must be met. Keep in mind that some of these criteria may not be the same in all countries. In the USA, show standards can be reviewed on the American Silkie Bantam Club website. While in the UK, it is the British poultry standard that is used.

If you look for a show silkie, you should buy silkies that match the standard of perfection and breed them together to end up with chicks that all the silkie lovers will admire. Most silkies in America are bantams. Both bearded and non-bearded silkies are accepted in shows in the US and Australia, while in the UK bearded silkies are better qualified. Naked-neck silkies go under the "all other varieties" of silkies.

Here are the main traits that an ideal show silkie should have. Note that these standard traits may slightly vary from one country to another. So, you need to get the exact standards from the official organization that has set them. Here are some of them:

1. Five toes and each toe is separate from the others.
2. Feathering that looks and feels furry.
3. Black skin.
4. Mulberry comb in cocks, round and visible in bearded silkie hens.
5. Blue turquoise ears, mulberry in cocks is allowed.
6. Dark brown eyes.
7. Appropriate size.
8. Dense feathering and undercoat has a pure white color.
9. Full toe feathering, the feathers on the feet should be on the middle toe and be soft and abundant like down.
10. Shredded appearance of wing feathers.
11. Soft and abundant tail feathers. Cocks should not have a flowing tail.
12. Round side appearance, square top appearance.
13. Smooth continuity of back saddle feathers and the tail

14. Fluffy round feathers around the hocks.

We highly recommend taking these criteria into consideration when you buy show silkies. Pet quality silkie chickens may be higher in price since they are selected to be chicken models. But you can buy chicks from the hatchery that perfectly matches the standard. But if you are merely looking for pet silkies regardless of their appearance, you can choose your own collection of colors and varieties and cross them to get wonderful chicks.

Do show silkies require special care and housing?

It is recommended not to have any fighting or pecking between chickens.

Good housing is extremely important and has a huge impact on chicken look and fitness. It is recommended to separate show silkie chickens from the rest of the flock and raise them separately because bullying and feather pecking can cause bad marks on feathers and skin that can result in getting them disqualified.

Show silkies should be kept in free range with precaution. Roaming in the dense grass can harm their feathers and tint them. So, avoid letting show silkies roam in dense or long grass to preserve their feather quality. The garden grass should be trimmed short to let them roam without getting their feathers damaged. Free range is good for chicken welfare.

Many silkie owners prefer to keep the silkies as house pets. This may not be safe for humans unless you keep a high biosecurity for you and your family.

Meeting the poultry standards

To meet the standards, you should raise and breed show quality silkies. These silkies can be bought from breeders who participate in shows and are known for getting prizes for their silkies.

The silkie show standards differ from one country to another. In shows, there are some points that are attributed for each body part based on some criteria:

✓ Weight

The weight is an important criterion. In US shows, it should be 36 oz. for cocks and 32 oz. for cockerels. The pullet should weigh 28 oz. and the hen 32 oz. In the UK, males should weigh 26 oz. and females 22 oz.

✓ Comb:

The comb should be walnut and circular in shape and broad with small prominences.

✓ Beak:

The beak should be short and firm with a laden blue color. The base of the beak should be broad.

✓ Eyes

The eyes should be black in color. They should look round, large and prominent.

✓ Wattles

Non-bearded silkies: the wattles should have a mulberry color. They should look round and have a medium size. They should be free from folds or wrinkles.

Bearded silkies: the wattles should look very small or absent.

✓ Ear lobes

They should look small and have a turquoise blue color.

✓ Head

The head should be small, and carried and slightly bypass the tip of the nails.

✓ Neck

The neck should be short or have a medium length and be broad at the base.

✓ Saddle

Should be broad, round, rising to the tail and have the silkiest feathers.

✓ Tail

The tail should be short and ragged at ends.

✓ Wings

The wing should be soft and fluffy at the shoulders

✓ Shanks

The shanks should be short, stout and well feathered.

✓ Colors

Only bearded white silkies are accepted in US qualification shows, whereas all the other colors are accepted in UK shows: blue, gold, white, partridge and black.

✓ Legs and toes

Legs should be short, stout and straight when viewed from the front. There should be 5 toes on each leg.

Getting ready for the show!

To get your silkies ready, they must look clean and fluffy. For that you need to examine their feathers and decide whether they need a simple brightening spray or consider bathing them to get clean feathers.

- Bathing

For bathing silkies, you can use a plastic pan. For silkies you need to use a specific shampoo suitable for your silkie color or a whitening shampoo.

1. Warm the water and wet down your silkie.
2. Mix the shampoo with water but still at a good concentration that it foams nicely.
3. Brush up the feathers nicely, making sure to cover all the feathers, gently brush the feathers of the legs and between the toes as well as the bum feathers.
4. Rinse the feathers.
5. Mix the shampoo with water and let it run for 3 minutes, be careful not to let it run too much so it can lighten the dye.
6. Rinse out the shampoo as much as possible.
7. Wrap your silkie up in a towel.
8. Dry her with a hair dryer and make sure she is all dry.

9. After your chicken is dry, brush the feathers gently with a slicker brush to remove any waxy feathers.
10. You can add coat lifter to their feathers and apply a transparent nail polish on the claws to make them shine. You can also add few sprays of perfume to the feathers.

- Clipping the nails

The nails also need to be trimmed and polished. To do this, you should be careful to cut a small portion of the nail edge about the last 1/5 of the nail. Try not to make the nail bleed. If you are new to this, you better be careful and ask experienced people for help. Polish the nail tip after clipping.

Chapter 9. Silkie Chicken's Health

Like all other pets, chickens can sometimes get sick. Diseases are caused by many factors and can come at whatever time, even when the chickens are well looked after and their living condition is excellent. It is important to keep in mind that diseases can be favored by the lack of hygiene in the coop or defects in the ventilation. Most of the diseases are caused by small bugs: bacteria and viruses and there are also some other factors that we will explain in this chapter.

Diseases in chickens can easily occur and transmit within the flock. So, you must make sure your flock is happy and healthy and not lose any of them owing to a lack of knowledge about feeding best practices or some defects in the coop design or the lack of good hygiene. It is important to keep in mind that veterinary consultations are necessary when one of your birds is sick because chickens do not respond well to diseases.

When chickens get sick, they exhibit a change in their behavior like loss of appetite or change in their normal activities. So, it is important for every chicken owner to regularly control chickens and have a closer look in their plumage and eyes, to make sure all is good. Ill chickens should be treated as soon as possible, because unlike other animals, ill chickens can soon die because their immune system is weak.

When the vet prescribes a drug, then a withdrawal time is necessary, that is the time after you stop using the medication that you must wait before you can eat the eggs from medicated birds. If you want to sell organic eggs, you cannot use most medications on the chickens producing them since this is a major infraction to being biologic.

Checking for signs of diseases

Ensuring your silkie chickens are in good shape and looking for signs of diseases is an important practice that pet owners should consider. The symptoms your silkie exhibits may indicate a slight or serious health problem. So how do you know when to call the vet? It is better to call the vet when any unusual signs appear to one of your chickens, diseases may be fatal and there may not be much time to save the sick chicken. You must visit the vet if any of the following general or specific symptoms occurs:

Symptoms can be general like signs of fatigue and drowsiness, dropping of wings or head, or no interest in food. Some other signs are related to a specific system like the digestive tract. So, if the chicken is wheezing, or panting, or having runny nostrils, these may indicate a respiratory infection. Lumps, rashes, or skin sores may indicate a skin problem or hernia. Diarrhea indicates a digestive or renal problem.

These symptoms can signal a disease and you must refer to your vet to get the sick chicken treated.

Choosing a vet

Your veterinarian is your partner who will help you ensure the flock is healthy. You will need the vet for vaccination and treatment of diseases. But not all vets get along well with chickens as there are many areas of practice for vets. There are large animal vets, canine vets, wildlife vets and avian vets. Obviously, you need to choose an avian vet to get more customized information and advice on how to raise and look after your chickens.

Whenever you have a question, pick up the phone and ask the vet. He will be glad to help. You can ask the vets about the silkie breed and if they are familiar with it. It is recommended that you schedule vaccination of chicks with your vet.

The vet check is crucial when it comes to diseases, many chickens get respiratory infections, or diarrhoea, or injuries that require medical care and sometimes surgery. In some areas, many vets are not interested in treating chickens, either because they are busy treating large animals or because they are not avian specialists. So, it is important for owners to have some remedies and disinfectants to use in case of known issues like wound management and parasite infections.

Unfortunately, many chicken owners use drugs without enough knowledge of how and when to use them. Be careful when self-medicating your chickens, you may harm your chickens unknowingly and make them worse. Always ask specialists before any treatment.

Injuries

Sometimes chickens get injured. Trauma results most commonly from predators' attacks including dogs, cats, and wild animals such as raccoons, weasels, possums, foxes, and larger birds of prey. Chicken fighting can also result in injuries. Injuries range from mild wounds to severe abrasions and bone fractures. Silkie hens can also get injured on their backs from aggressive rooster mating. They present with missing feathers and abrasions in their back or neck. Dominant chickens peck at chickens further down the pecking order, often plucking out feathers and causing bleeding wounds that attract more pecking from other flock mates. Predator wounds are usually more severe and located around the neck or wings. Due to their dense feathers, wounds may sometimes be masked, injuries to wings and legs are more obvious as they may show signs of limp or fallen wings. If the chicken gets attacked by predators, she may be in shock and this requires rehydration, warmth, and administration of pain relievers. There are many commercial disinfectants for use in case of wounds. Pharmaceutical honey also works well for wound healing and can be used.

When there is intense bleeding, you must stop the bleeding. Use a gauze sponge and apply pressure to the injury for a few minutes. This will help stop the bleeding. Then clear feathers away from the affected area or trim them if necessary. Spray the wound abundantly with an antiseptic solution such as a dilute Dakin's solution to flush away debris. Apply a bandage to prevent the wound infection. Repeat these steps 2 or 3 times a day and keep the chicken in a safe place until the wound heals.

If the wound has a deep pouch, this may be a big problem. It may result in the infection of the pouch and formation of an abscess. If there is a skin laceration, take your chicken to the vet as this may require sutures.

In addition to the local treatment of the wound, antibiotic shots or pills must be given to prevent the wound infection and sepsis. It is important to assess the wound healing daily. If the wound is getting swollen or taking too long to heal, you'd better take your chicken to the vet. Injured birds should be separated from the rest of the flock until the wound heals properly to avoid pecking. If the wound is more than 2 days old, it may show some evidence of green bruising. In some cases when there is a lot of damage to the internal structures of the abdomen or the chest and the wound is incorrigible, it is better to put the chicken down to end his suffering.

The crook neck

Many silkie breeders have seen this condition in silkie chicks. The skull on the top of their head makes the brain vulnerable to painful accidents with severe consequences.

Some silkies do not show signs of the hernia through their entire life, some are affected from an early age and can be spotted a few days after hatching. This may be of no consequences most of the time, but there may be some neurological signs that some birds may show, like permanent deformity of the neck or crook neck. Others recover with a permanent tilt to the head and the chick cannot lift his head anymore. Others do not survive as they cannot feed or drink and die of dehydration.

It is good practice to minimize the big skull vault in your flock. Crossing vaulted silkies with non-vaulted silkies makes this trait less likely to occur in chicks. Sometimes, breeding two vaulted skull silkies together can be fatal for the future litter. The chicks are more likely to die during incubation or after hatching and getting head injuries.

Good raising matters a lot in helping chicks overcome this critical period; if you keep chicks in a good area and provide them with enough food and water, the problem may go unnoticed. The vaulted skull may be the only down side of silkies as a breed as they are gentle and make lovely pets. So, care must be taken before buying silkies and when intending to breed them.

If the brain gets hit hard, it may get inflamed. The inflammation produces fluid which can create a compression to the brain. It is called water on the brain. It usually hits young birds but can happen at any age. It often happens when chicks are crowded, especially with more aggressive breeds in the mix.

Symptoms include walking backwards and falling over. The bird may spin around in circles, fall over or lie on his back unable to walk, shows a crooked neck or is unable to stand and walk. It is quite painful and most of the time it ends in death. This condition may be confused with a vitamin deficiency, group B vitamins and vitamin E.

Vets usually give a shot of a steroid anti-inflammatory like prednisone to alleviate the pain with some vitamin pills. A daily administration of prednisone and vitamins is necessary with assisted feeding. Birds with severe cases of crook neck can't eat and drink enough to survive. So, use a syringe to feed them. Make sure they drink a lot of water with some sugar and salt.

Many vitamin supplements can be used like Polyvisol drops, ¼ of dropperful in the morning and in the evening, if not available. Use Selenium tablets and vitamin E capsules, vitamin B complex pills and electrolyte powder to put in her water. Be cautious and respect the dosage. If you do exceed the dosage, the bird can become intoxicated.

Contact your vet to know the perfect dose. If the chicken responds to the vitamin cure, then he was probably suffering from a nutritional deficiency. But if the problem persists, you will have to continue with prednisone for a long period of time. The Prednisone dosage should be gradually decreased and should not be stopped abruptly.

If the treatment is stopped, the water is likely to form again and pressure builds in the skull making symptoms reappear again. If you and your bird are lucky, hand feeding and the vitamins will be all that is needed. But sometimes things can go the other way. In these cases, vets recommend euthanasia to stop the suffering. Euthanasia may be a traumatic decision for your beloved silkie, but it is sometimes the kindest way to stop the bird suffering.

It is recommended not to breed silkies with big head knobs to avoid these types of problems.

Diarrhea

Chicken poop is an important health indicator, and it is one of the first signs of diseases. Normal chicken poop has a pasty consistency with some transparent liquid that comes with it. It has a smelly rancid odor. Loose droppings are quite normal for chickens.

Diarrhea is a common chicken symptom that occurs in young chicks as well as adults. Diarrhea is basically recognized when hens are having dirty wet vents or stained eggs. The feathers around the vent become matted.

In some cases, the gut gets infected and the absorption decreases. The chicken becomes dehydrated and weak. It is important to rehydrate him and treat the underlying cause.

Diarrhea results in chicken droppings becoming like liquid. The color may not be a good indicator, since normal chicken poop color comes in a wide range of brown, yellow, green or black. The poop color is related to the diet, but in most cases, it is brownish with a small white proportion that is always present.

Diarrhea in chickens has many causes. It may be infectious: consecutive to a gut infection with bacteria or with gut parasites. It may also be due to renal problems. In chicks, diarrhea can be mainly caused by pathogen bacteria like E. Coli or an infection with Gumboro's disease virus. Gut worms and coccidia can also cause diarrhea. Coccidiosis is a common parasitic infestation that leads to blood stained diarrhea.

The color of the diarrheic poop may sometimes serve in determining the cause. Your vet needs a complete history of the diarrhea as well as a poop analysis to determine the cause. Knowing the cause of the diarrhea is the key to the success of its treatment.

Diarrhea results in dehydration and electrolyte imbalance. Beside antibiotics or antiparasitic drugs, the chicken will need a large volume of water and electrolytes to compensate the loss due to the diarrhea. Ensuring the chicken drinks enough water with salt and sugar is extremely helpful. It is important to separate the sick individuals from the rest of the flock. Give them their medicines daily until symptoms regress.

Runny nostrils

Chickens are extremely susceptible to respiratory infections. The respiratory system of chickens is prone to many diseases. So, a silkie keeper should keep the coop isolated from air flow and minimize dust.

There are many bacteria and viruses that infect the sinuses, the trachea and the lungs and cause her to have nostril discharge. Affected chickens will show many symptoms like panting, struggling to breath and drooling. When you notice any of these signs, quickly separate the affected birds to help block the transmission of the infection to the rest of the flock. This will help control the spread of the infection. The bird should be treated for some days with antibiotics and anti-inflammatories.

There are many respiratory diseases. Many of them mimic each other in terms of symptoms. Most respiratory infections are caused by viruses, and there are no active drugs that can kill viruses.

Treatment is based on antibiotics and anti-inflammatories to avoid bacterial infection. Some natural oils help relieve the congestion that can be used such as vetrx, which can be rubbed on their nostrils.

Existing respiratory diseases within a flock can last for a long time. The virus can be shed in feeders and waterers and can continuously infect chicks. So, a good disinfection of the coop helps reduce the viral load.

Many parameters can favour the onset of respiratory problems such as the lack and the excess of ventilation, fierce winds, excess of dust and wild bird contact. Caution should be taken to protect the coop against violent air flow, especially in the freezing weather.

Egg binding

Sometimes, silkie hens have trouble laying eggs. The hen will have a hard time walking and stops eating. The bound egg could be seen in the cloaca. Obese hens are likely to develop bound eggs. This may happen because of an excessively large egg. An egg with a double yolk in silkies may be a cause.

In some cases, the egg has a good size but the cloaca does not push the egg out enough. This may be caused by a decrease in blood Calcium levels or a traumatized vent. The vet should undertake treatment of this condition with lubricating the egg canal and attempt to ease the egg out. If this doesn't work, the egg may be crushed and the contents are extracted. In some cases, when the condition is late to be identified, the uterus can get infected. Some vets perform surgery to extract the uterus. Calcium supplementation may be necessary.

Nutritional disorders

Nutritional disorders are quite common in chickens, they are mainly due to errors in diet formulation of chickens. Most disorders result from nutritional deficiencies rather than excess of nutrients. Deficiencies often concern trace elements like vitamins and minerals.

Vitamin deficiency

Vitamins are required for chickens in limited amounts. With an insufficient amount the body can get diseases and it may lead to death if not well treated. Chickens must obtain their dosage of vitamins through the food. The concentration of vitamins in foods is different from one item to another, that's why it is important to feed a diet that has different components.

Vitamin and mineral deficiencies usually occur in chickens which are fed on one or two food items. The table below lists vitamin roles and deficiency symptoms. Although the symptoms are not specifically related to vitamin deficiency, it may be helpful to know some of them. It is important to keep in mind that when chickens show one of these symptoms, to take your vet advice. It can be a more serious health problem that needs vet intervention.

- Vitamin A deficiency

Chicks given diets deficient in vitamin A will show poor growth and bad feathers. In advanced stages, they may become unable to stand. They will have dry and red eyes with the presence of yellow material beneath the eyelids. Laying hens subjected to vitamin A deficiency will have a poor egg quality and sometimes blood spots on them. Since vitamin A protects respiratory and gut mucosa, infections may occur on those sites.

- Vitamin D3 Deficiency

Since vitamin D helps build bones, a deficiency will lead to rickets in immature flocks. As it is a condition with bone deformities, young birds show an unwillingness to walk. Swellings of the joints may also be noted and a decreased growth rate and bad feathers, too.

- Vitamin E Deficiency

Vitamin E is required in complex biochemical functions and it is fast oxidized in chicken feeds. Deficiencies may occur with chickens fed with old feeds or out of date feed. The presence of free radicals will result in the destruction of vitamin E. Deficiency results in a condition known as encephalomalacia and chicks shown neurological signs.

Calcium and Phosphorus deficiency

Calcium and phosphorus are essential minerals to animals' bodies and especially for chickens. They are associated with bone formation and egg shell formation. Deficiencies in Calcium and phosphorus cause rickets in chicks. In hens, this will reduce egg production and sometimes the production of eggs without shells. Since Calcium is involved in muscle contraction, deficiencies can result in weakness.

Parasites

Parasites are small creatures that colonize chicken bodies and feed on the body tissues like skin, feathers, blood and intestinal content. Parasites can live inside the body, these are called ectoparasites and there are some others that live inside the body. Many parasites are visible and some others are extra small that cannot be seen with the naked eye. Parasites belong to many families like insects to which flies and acarines like mites and ticks belong. Internal parasites are mainly gut parasites, these are worms that live in the intestines and in the windpipe.

Skin and feather lice

Lice are small arthropods that infest many domestic animals including chickens and they are responsible for a big discomfort for chickens. There are many types of lice that feed on the blood, the skin or the feathers.

Lice live attached to the body and benefit from the warmth of the skin to thrive and reproduce. A small number of lice is not remarkably harmful, but when their number becomes bigger, lice can cause a lot of damage in your pen, especially blood sucking ones. They cause anemia and weakness. They spend their entire life cycle on the chicken.

More than 40 species of lice have been identified in domestic fowl. Wild birds carry lice. In young chicks, lice are very annoying. They feed on skin debris and provoke discomfort. Lice can be easily seen with the naked eye and are yellowish in color and flat-bodied.

Lice species vary in the preferred area of the body they infect. There are body lice, head lice and feather lice. Their transmission occurs via close contact with infested chickens. Many chicken owners struggle to treat lice, they often come back again for chickens.

If you want to successfully control lice, follow a good treatment plan that consists of treating chickens, their coop, as well as the environment they live in. Don't only think to spray chemicals on your chickens. This may not be efficient since lice can be found everywhere and they can crawl to reach the chickens.

Treatment options for lice are variable. There are many commercial products that help kill lice, they are available in many forms: sprays, dusting powder etc. Dusting powders seem to be the most effective treatment since it is added in the dusting area. When the birds do their dust bath, the chemical reaches their skin and kills the lice. But this procedure is not effective in roosters as they dust themselves much less often, it may be necessary to treat roosters with other measures like sprays.

Acaricide sprays are also a good choice. They must be applied to the whole flock. It is important not to exceed the prescribed dosage to avoid toxicity. Sprays must be applied twice a day to completely eradicate lice. The reason is that most acaricides are active against adult lice and not eggs. So, when first applied to the skin, lice eggs escape being killed and hatch and they will infest chickens again. So, it is important to repeat the treatment 2 weeks later to get a full recovery.

It is important to know that every acaricide has a period in which it stays active and may be excreted in eggs. Care should be taken not to consume any eggs in the prescribed period. You should follow label directions for withdrawal times.

Some acaricides are sold as concentrates that need to be diluted in water before use. Make sure you make the right dosage before use and keep the acaricide away from children and other pets. For your safety, dust powders are a better choice. They are more active and require no manipulation.

Ivermectin is a famous anti parasitic drug but it is less effective in treating lice. A few drops on the back of the neck may help control the infection.

Another new treatment is based on the use of probiotics; these are bacteria that help treat lice by producing toxic substances that kill them. There are some ointments that contain specific bacteria like "Bacillus thuringiensis" that produce a lousicide substance called "thuringiensin". These products are claimed to be effective and they are good to try since they are less likely to cause intoxication for chickens and have no withdrawal time. These products may not be available on the market.

The coop and its equipment need to be treated also, since they will continue to shed the parasites. So, you should clean the coop and apply insecticides on it. Spray the acaricide on perches and on the nests.

Mites

Mites are tiny arthropods that are much smaller than lice. Most of them can't be seen with the naked eye. Mites feed on blood, feathers, and skin. They affect chickens, ducks, geese and wild birds. Mites can spend their entire life on chickens. Some others can also leave their host and hide in the environment.

Treatment of mites involves treating the environment as well as chickens. Some mites, such as red skin mites, live on their host at night. They feed at night when chickens sleep and during the day. They hide in cracks and joints of the coop; therefore, you can't see them. Some mites can survive in the environment for a long time without food.

More commonly encountered mite species include the chicken mite, the northern fowl mite and the scaly leg mite.

- Chicken red mites

Red mites are blood sucking parasites with a reddish color. It is common on both chickens and other fowl species and some birds. Red mites are hardly spotted because they are active at night and hide in the day. Red mites spend most of their life in small crevices and cracks of the coop.

Humans occasionally get infested with red mites. Mite infestation results in wrecked feathers and the peaking behavior, restlessness and loss of condition. Heavy infestations can result in a decrease of egg production and weight loss. Mites can be transferred via fomites including crates, cages, clothing, and wild birds.

Dust boxes containing sand and either diatomaceous earth (DE) or kaolin clay, reduce the infestation. Dichlorvos, Malathion dust and garlic oil are effective in the treatment of mites in chickens followed by Ivermectin which is also commonly used.

Treatment in poultry appears to be effective.

It is important to regularly check the chickens for parasites and the chickens' house and perches for these parasites. Attention must be paid not to allow any crevices or cracks in chickens' houses, as they are known to harbor mites.

- Scaly leg mites

Scaly leg mites are parasites located on the leg. When massively infested, legs show a crust of loose white tissue with an intense itching. It can result in serious damage to the leg. The parasites infest the chickens and infiltrate under the scales of their legs. They feed on the tissues and burrow into the skin. The skin is inflamed and the scales are therefore uplifted.

The scaly leg infection results in a crusty lesion that is installed on the feet and the legs. Parasites reproduce inside tunnels under the skin. Older chickens are commonly more affected than young ones.

Treatment is based on using acaricides. Use Vaseline ointment to soften roughened scales. Although it is not licensed for chickens. Ivermectin 1% spot on drops are good to use.

Another treatment consists of dipping the chicken legs in a solution of diluted acaricide twice a week. The coop should be also treated because mites can hide in the environment and return to infest other animals.

Acaricides require a withdrawal period for eggs; the eggs are not safe to eat or to sell. It may take quite a long time for the legs to heal properly and regenerate new scales. This period may take a few months. It is recommended to wash the legs using commercial shampoo and a toothbrush once every 2 weeks. This will help keep legs clean and healthy. Regular control of legs is necessary.

Internal parasites

- Gapeworms

A gapeworm (Syngamus trachea) also known as a red worm and forked worm is a nematode worm that infects the trachea. Adult worms lay eggs in the trachea that are passed up the trachea and swallowed, they are then released with feces. They contaminate the soil and infect other chickens. Signs include gaping and gasping.

- Crop worms

These are long and slender nematodes that are embedded in the crop mucosa. They are known as threadworms and are less than 60mm long. These nematodes lay eggs that are shed in the feces. The ova may infest a second host or just stay in the environment to mature. It takes a month for an egg to become an adult threadworm.

- Roundworms or Ascaridiasis

Roundworms reside in the small intestine of chickens. They infest young chicks as early as 3 months of age. The eggs are excreted in feces and infect other chickens. Infected birds will have a poor condition and may have diarrhea. If the infection is intense, mortality can occur.

The control of internal parasites is based on the use of anthelminthic drugs. Piperazine is an effective treatment. Fenbendazole and Levamisole should not be used for layer hens since they are excreted in eggs and eggs are not safe to eat or sell. The use of natural deworming agents like pumpkin seeds, Cayene pepper, Garlic and cucumbers are good to use. Deworming should be repeated on a monthly or bimonthly basis.

Viral diseases

There is a branch of diseases that are caused by viruses. Viruses are the smallest living-like entities that cause diseases in humans and animals. Most devastating diseases are caused by viruses, first because viruses reproduce fast, second, they have intelligent mechanisms to hide inside the body and third because there are not enough drugs that act against viruses. AIDS, Ebola, and Rabies are human diseases that are caused by viruses. Even the most devastating chicken diseases are caused by viruses, such as avian influenza, Newcastle disease and Marek's disease.

Newcastle disease

Newcastle disease is a contagious and fatal viral disease affecting all species of birds, including chickens. The virus infects chickens and reproduces fast in the body and many chickens die without having shown any signs. Newcastle signs are not specific and in most cases, they are not indicative of the disease. Veterinarians use autopsy to diagnose it.

The disease is transmitted within the air between chickens and can be introduced to the flock from wild birds. The Newcastle disease virus may cause conjunctivitis in humans.

There is no treatment for Newcastle disease but there is vaccination. If there is a previous exposure to the virus in backyard flocks, then vaccination is necessary. The vaccine is administered in the water.

Marek's Disease

Marek's disease is very common in chickens. It is highly contagious and it is transmitted through the air. It can also be transmitted by the feathers of sick chickens. Once a bird is infected, the virus remains indefinitely in his body and that's what causes the persistence of the disease within the flock. Signs of the disease are subtle and include weight loss, loss of appetite and diarrhea as well as neurological signs. There may be an enlargement of feather follicles.

There is no known treatment for Marek's disease. Prevention is implemented through acquisition of vaccinated chickens from reputable breeders.

Avian Influenza

Avian influenza is a highly contagious disease that is caused by a virus similar to the flu virus of humans. The avian influenza is rare in backyard flocks. Migratory birds can pose a threat to backyard chickens. The disease is associated with respiratory signs like sneezing, cough and rattling. The virus is spread in the air and can infect other chickens.

Due to its similarity with influenza viruses of other species, this virus can spread from waterfowl to chickens and from pigs to chickens and from humans to turkeys. The world has known many epidemies of avian influenza and they had mild consequences. There is no cure for the avian influenza, vaccination is not usually practiced.

Fowl pox

Fowl pox is a highly contagious skin infection caused by a virus. It affects most species of birds. It affects chickens and most commonly the unfeathered portions of the head or neck with formation of scabs on the skin, combs, wattles, and inside the mouth and sometimes it occurs on the feet or vent.

Fowl pox can be transmitted by direct or indirect contact between chickens. The desquamated scabs can also infect other chickens and remain infectious in the environment for many months. The disease can also be transmitted by flying insects. Fowl pox infection results in weight loss and drop in egg production.

The treatment of this disease is only supportive and vaccines are the best way to protect the flock from the infection. Affected chickens should be isolated from the rest of the flock and treated.

Birds should be given painkillers to drop the elevated body temperature. Use gloves to imbibe the infected portions of the skin in Vaseline to soften the scabs, then apply an antiseptic solution like diluted Iodine or Methylen blue solution to prevent their infection. Some vets do shots of antibiotics to prevent the infection of the scabs.

If the chicken is reluctant to eat, it's important to make him drink plenty of fluids to avoid dehydration. Cleaning the coop as well as mosquito control should be undertaken to minimize the spread of the infection.

Avian encephalomyelitis

Encephalomyelitis is a viral disease that can affect chicks at a very young age. Affected chickens will show weakness, tremors of the head, neck and feet as well as a decrease in egg production. The infection is hardly diagnosed within a flock of chickens since it may not give specific lesions. Prevention is based on vaccination.

Bacterial diseases

Salmonellosis

Salmonellosis is a zoonotic bacterial disease that may be transmitted to humans from contaminated food, including eggs. Many species of domestic animals can shed the bacteria including chickens. The bacteria live in the intestine and chickens may not show any symptoms. Salmonella can be excreted in feces and survives in poultry litter for quite a long time.

It is essential for chicken keepers to wash their hands with soap and water after handling chickens. It is estimated that 1.4 million annual cases of human salmonellosis occur in the US. In chickens, salmonellosis can cause mortality, anorexia, white diarrhea, and poor feathering.

It is recommended not to treat any cases of salmonellosis. There are fears from bacterial resistance that could threaten humans. Affected flocks should be eliminated, not to infect humans.

Mycoplasmosis

Mycoplasmosis is a chronic respiratory disease due to Mycoplasma. It can be transmitted by direct contact between chickens and from infected parents to progeny through the egg as well as from wild birds. Mycoplasma infection causes ocular discharge, wheezing and it affects chicken growth. Mycoplasmosis may cause arthritis of the hock and stifle joint.

Treatment is based on the use of antibiotics. Tylosin in drinking water is an effective cure.

Behavioral disorders

Egg eating

Chickens may occasionally develop a habit of eating their own or other hen's eggs. This behavior is difficult to stop once it has started. This behavior is thought to be the result of overcrowding, lack of nests, nutritional deficiency, or the presence of cracked eggs in the chicken coop, either by predators or intentionally given in chicken feed.

There are many tricks used by chicken owners to stop this behavior. A solution consists of gathering the eggs as soon as possible from the nests to prevent the hens from cracking them and enjoying their deliciousness.

There are many tricks to stop egg eating. Some of which consist of placing white stones the size of the egg or golf balls in the nest, or using an egg filled with something that has a bitter taste and placing it back into the nest can also work. The egg can be emptied by poking a small hole in each end of the egg and blowing on one end. Next, the egg is filled up with dish-soap or mustard so that when the hen cracks the egg she will be disappointed by the new taste. This method works fine. Making the nest dark may sometimes help reducing egg eating.

Vent pecking

Vent pecking is rare to happen among layer hens when their nests are not enough dark. It is basically because chickens like to pick up shiny things or red things. Just after laying the egg, the hen's cloaca protrudes a little bit from the vent. The uncovered red tissue attracts attention and pecking from other chickens.

This condition can be due to a lack of Calcium in the chicken feed. Calcium helps muscle contraction. If the diet is deficient in Calcium, the cloaca muscle contraction becomes slower and sometimes incomplete. That's what makes it visible for a longer period and the hens are likely to peck each others vents. The victim can be seriously injured and even disemboweled.

Show silkies should be raised in a stress-free environment and never let this happen because they will be disqualified. For pet chickens, to prevent this condition, you have to use blinders or peepers. These are plastic devices that a chicken wears on her face to partially block her vision and prevent her from bullying her flock mates. There are also anti-peck sprays that can be applied to feathers to stop this phenomenon.

Abnormal egg production

Good healthy eggs of silkies are white/ white brown. Eggshells should be clean and not containing any dirt. In some cases, eggs can have an abnormal color or have some precipitate. This condition reflects the hen's health. If you notice any change in color, or when eggs have some blood clots, don't hesitate to ask your vet for help.

It is important to consume cooked eggs so that any eventual bacteria are killed. It is important to keep in mind that when you are using drugs to treat chickens, a withdrawal period is necessary to help the chicken body get rid of the drugs and so that they are not secreted in eggs. Eggs should only be consumed after a withdrawal period. The table below lists most common egg abnormalities and their explication:

Problem	Causes
Pale-shelled Eggs	<ul><li>Common in very old hens.</li><li>Respiratory infections</li><li>Stress.</li><li>Use of some drugs.</li></ul>
Pink Eggs	<ul><li>Excess calcium in the feed.</li><li>Stress.</li></ul>
Dirty Eggs:	<ul><li>Diarrhoea, wet droppings due to feed that contains excess of moist like fruits).</li><li>Indigestible compounds in feed</li><li>Saline water.</li><li>Kidney disease.</li></ul>
Blood stained eggs	<ul><li>Pullets are fat or coming into lay.</li><li>Poor hygiene in the coop.</li><li>Prolapsed cloaca.</li><li>Vent pecking.</li></ul>
Shell-less Eggs:	<ul><li>Shell gland problem.</li><li>Due to some diseases: like Newcastle's or avian influenza.</li><li>Imbalanced diet: lack of minerals or Vitamin D3.</li></ul>
Soft-shelled Eggs	<ul><li>Occurs in very old hens.</li><li>Excess phosphorus in the diet.</li><li>Heat stress.</li><li>Saline water.</li></ul>
Cracks	<ul><li>Heat stress.</li><li>Saline water.</li><li>Poor nutrition, especially calcium and vitamin D3.</li></ul>
Calcium Deposits	<ul><li>Defective shell gland.</li></ul>

	<ul><li>Disturbances during calcification.</li><li>Poor nutrition, e.g. Excess calcium.</li></ul>
Misshaped Eggs	<ul><li>Shell gland problem.</li><li>Disease: Newcastle disease, infectious bronchitis, Laryngotracheitis.</li><li>Stress.</li><li>Over-crowding.</li></ul>

Chapter 10. Frequently Asked Questions

- How to break a hen's broodiness?

There are various ways to break this broodiness. One option is to place the hen in a wire-bottomed cage away from the flock for several days. Broody silkies can bite so wear gloves when you're doing this. Give her food and water and regularly inspect her feet because these cages can cause feet injuries.

- How long do chickens live?

Chickens live quite a long time, if they are healthy and live in stress-free environment. Chickens can live up to 10 years.

- What to feed show silkies?

Silkies kept as show pets can be fed normal layer pellets, which gives them a balanced diet. Supplements and vitamin mix are not necessary unless the diet is deficient. Grit is needed if your chickens are free range. You can feed your silkies table scraps, fruits, vegetables, bugs and seeds, pasta, rice, cooked potato, broccoli, fish, cucumber, watermelon, cooked eggs, bread and they love meal worms.

- How old do silkies need to be shown at a show?

Shows are dedicated for mature silkies. Chickens mature at 20 to 24 weeks.

- Why is my hen losing feathers?

Outside molting season, broody hens tend to pluck their own breast feathers out so their skin is in direct contact with the eggs. You can prevent this by adding soft bedding to the nest.

Over-mating also results in saddle feather loss in hens. The rooster plucks up the saddle feathers of hens to stabilize her. This is completely different from molting. You can stop that by attaching a hen apron, which is clothing that protects their backs from roosters during mating. Increasing the number of hens is helpful to reduce the over-mating.

- How to prepare chickens for winter?

If the weather in winter is extremely cold, then silkies can get cold and there may be frostbite. This must not happen is show quality silkies. Try to make the coop warmer by adding thick insulated walls and roof. Caution should be taken to allow air to circulate inside the coop.

- Why aren't my chickens laying eggs?

Chickens stop laying when they are at the molting period. Egg laying may be reduced in winter because there is less daylight. It is not something to worry about, it is rather normal in these cases. When egg drop occurs in the spring, check the hen's body condition and watch for signs of diseases and bound eggs. Egg drop is a common symptom in many diseases and it has many causes.

Great chicken websites

It is a good idea for a silkie keeper to ask questions and share his knowledge with experienced chicken keepers. The Internet is very enriching and you can get support from many active associations of chickens. There are plenty of groups about silkie chickens.

Joining a group allows you to read advice from other silkie owners. Some groups are solely online, others are by mail, and a few are groups that regularly meet.

- The American Silkie Bantam Club:

Http://www.americansilkiebantamclub.org

It is the original Silkie Club in the US. It is devoted to raising and breeding silkies. Gives valuable information for show breeders and pet breeders. It has a forum and any one can join this organization.

- Silkie Exhibitors and Breeders of America:

Http://www.sebaclub.com

A new Silkie Club in the USA which is exclusively dedicated to encouraging the breeding and exhibiting of show quality Silkies.

- American Poultry Association:

Http://www.amerpoultryassn.com

The APA promotes and protects the standard-bred poultry industry and continues the publication of the American Standard of Perfection with the breed and variety descriptions for all the recognized purebred fowl.

- National Silkie Breeders Association

Http://nationalsilkieba.weebly.com

- The Silkie Club of Great Britain:

Http://thesilkieclub.weebly.com

The SCGB provides useful information on how to show, breed or just keep silkies as pets. It was founded in 1898.

- Silkie Club of Australia:

www.Silkieclubofaustralia.webs.com

- The Silkie Club of New Zealand:

Http://newzealandsilkieclub.weebly.com

This page includes the Silkie standards for New Zealand.

- Silkie Breeders Yahoo Group:

Http://groups.yahoo.com/group/silkiebreeders

This is for breeders and exhibitors. This list is for serious silkie breeders and people interested in exhibition.

- The Awesome Silkie Bantam Chat:

Http://groups.yahoo.com/group/asbc

This is a large friendly list with an extensive archive. This group is a good source of information for beginners.

- The Backyard chickens site

Https://www.backyardchickens.com

Backyardchickens.com is a resourceful forum about chicken keeping. It contains contributions from chicken owners that may help you get an idea and learn tricks that other chicken keepers do.

www.ingramcontent.com/pod-product-compliance
Lightning Source LLC
Chambersburg PA
CBHW071450030726
47593CB00003B/969